WHERE DID I LEAVE MY GLASSES?

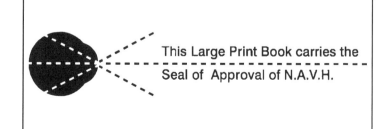

This Large Print Book carries the
Seal of Approval of N.A.V.H.

WHERE DID I LEAVE MY GLASSES?

THE WHAT, WHEN, AND WHY OF *Normal* MEMORY LOSS

MARTHA WEINMAN LEAR

THORNDIKE PRESS

A part of Gale, Cengage Learning

GALE
CENGAGE Learning

Detroit • New York • San Francisco • New Haven, Conn • Waterville, Maine • London

GALE
CENGAGE Learning

Copyright © 2008 by Martha Weinman Lear.
Thorndike Press, a part of Gale, Cengage Learning.

Thorndike Press® Large Print Nonfiction.
The text of this Large Print edition is unabridged.
Other aspects of the book may vary from the original edition.
Set in 16 pt. Plantin.
Printed on permanent paper.

LIBRARY OF CONGRESS CATALOGING-IN-PUBLICATION DATA

Lear, Martha Weinman.
    Where did I leave my glasses? : the what, when, and why of normal memory loss / by Martha Weinman Lear.
        p. cm.
    ISBN-13: 978-1-4104-0536-4 (hardcover : lg print)
    ISBN-10: 1-4104-0536-2 (hardcover : lg print)
    1. Memory in old age — Popular works. 2. Large type books.
    I. Title.
    BF724.85.M45L43 2009
    155.67'13125—dc22   2007048832

Published in 2008 by arrangement with Grand Central Publishing, a division of Hachette Book Group USA, Inc.

Printed in the United States of America
1 2 3 4 5 6 7 12 11 10 09 08

4/08 Pur.

FOR WHATSISNAME
(I think it begins with an *A*)

CONTENTS

ACKNOWLEDGMENTS

Reading what has been written by the best and brightest in their fields is all to the good, and I've done plenty of it. But that is not where the juice is. The juice is in the face-to-face interview, the spontaneous Q & A, the conversational detours that lead off the main road and around the bend and through the woods and into a sudden clearing where the view is terrific.

I have been doing magazine journalism for more than four decades, written scores of articles, interviewed hundreds of people, and this is a thing I learned long ago. Nothing — not the books and scientific journals, not the research papers, not the e-mail exchanges, not the glorious and (to me) incomprehensible know-it-all-ness of Google — *nothing* is as good as sitting down together in a room and letting it go where it will.

There have been many interviews with

many specialists in the course of preparing this book, and almost all of them have been done in just that way. A few, for one logistical reason or another, had to be conducted by telephone — not ideal but at least there are live voices and spontaneity. I am grateful to them all, and want especially to thank the following for their time and their expertise:

Simon Baron-Cohen, PhD, professor of developmental psychopathology, University of Cambridge; director of the Autism Research Centre of the department of psychiatry, University of Cambridge, England

Michal Schnaider Beeri, PhD, assistant professor of psychiatry, Mount Sinai School of Medicine, New York, NY

Rodney Brooks, PhD, professor of robotics and former director of the Computer Science and Artificial Intelligence Laboratory, Massachusetts Institute of Technology, Cambridge

Terrence Deacon, PhD, professor of biological anthropology, University of California, Berkeley

Gayatri Devi, MD, clinical associate professor of neurology and psychiatry, New York University School of Medicine; director, the New York Memory Services

Adam Gazzaley, MD, PhD, professor of neurology and physiology; director of the Neuroscience Imaging Center, University of California, San Francisco

Judy Illes, PhD, professor of neurology and Canada Research Chair in neuroethics, University of British Columbia, Vancouver

William Jagust, MD, professor of public health and neuroscience, University of California, Berkeley

Arthur F. Kramer, PhD, professor of neuroscience and psychology, University of Illinois at Urbana-Champaign

Richard E. Powers, MD, chairman of the scientific advisory committee of the Alzheimer's Foundation

Norman Relkin, MD, PhD, associate professor of clinical neurology and neuroscience; director of the Cornell Memory Disorders Program, Weill Cornell Medical College, New York-Presbyterian Hospital

Daniel L. Schacter, PhD, William R. Kenan, Jr., Professor of Psychology, Harvard University

Margaret Sewell, PhD, assistant clinical professor of psychiatry; director of the Memory Enhancement Program, Mount Sinai School of Medicine, New York, NY

Jeremy M. Silverman, PhD, professor of

psychiatry, Mount Sinai School of Medicine, New York, NY

David Sinclair, PhD, associate professor of pathology, Harvard Medical School

Meir Stampfer, DrPh, PhD, professor of nutrition and epidemiology, Harvard School of Public Health

Most of all, I am indebted to Dr. Barry Gordon, therapeutic cognitive neuroscience professor, and founder of the Memory Clinic at Johns Hopkins Medical Institutions in Baltimore; and to Dr. Yaakov Stern, professor of clinical neuropsychology at the Columbia University Medical Center in New York, and head of the Memory Disorders Center at the New York State Psychiatric Institute.

Both have been helpful beyond words — but that is precisely the point: words. Both know how to put the juice into the expertise. It is a rare and lovely gift, and I have been the lucky beneficiary.

M.W.L.

INTRODUCTION
BUT FIRST (AND BEFORE I FORGET) . . .

It is a comfort — not total, but I'll take whatever I can get — to know that we're all in this together, complaining more about remembering less.

I say *all* advisedly. It does not mean everyone. It means *us:* those of us who keep forgetting people's names or where we put the car keys or what we were just about to say. It means those of us who keep having those moments that are called, in the fullness of our American genius for euphemism, tip-of-the-tongue moments. If you are not yet plagued by such moments, you shouldn't be reading this book. It is not for you. Yet.

As for *us:* Let me tell you that, tip-of-the-tongue-wise, we are the world. The Italians say, *"Sulla punta della lingua."* The Spaniards say, *"Al punto de la lengua."* The French, who usually do not like sounding like everyone else, sound just like everyone else when they say, *"Sur le bout de la langue."* The Swedes say, *"Jag har det på tungan."* The Croatians say, *"Na vrhu jezika mi je,"* and the Dutch say, *"Op het puntje van mijn tong,"* though God knows how either of them pronounces it, and — here's the point — they are all describing *exactly* the same sensation in *exactly* the same way. In Japan, it's the same maddening sensation, but lower down. They say, "のど まで でかかってるんだけど," meaning "it's stuck in the throat."

This cheers me. Not that forgetfulness in itself is a rib tickler — not, at least, to those of us who do the forgetting — but I do find something intrinsically funny in the idea of a global chorus wailing, "What was I just going to say? *It's on the tip of my tongue.*" How's that for a babel of tongues?

Consider our own memory situations, yours and mine. Here is mine:

Adjectives elude me. Verbs escape me. Nouns, especially proper nouns, totally defeat me. I may meet you at a party, have a long, lovely conversation with you, be charmed by you, want to know you forever, and a day later not remember your name. (Do not feel offended. It is not your problem. However, if *you* do not remember *my* name, I promise you that I will feel offended.)

Often I cannot remember what I had for

dinner last night, never mind what my husband and I discussed while we ate it. But I can report with reasonable accuracy that our dinner table conversations, these days, proceed more or less like this.

"I started to tell you something."

"What?"

"I can't remember."

Or:

"I saw Whatsisname today."

"Who?"

"*You* know. *Whats*isname."

"Oh. Where?"

Or:

"Remember I asked you to be sure to remind me to call someone?"

"Yes."

"Who was it?"

"I forgot."

Or:

"What was I just looking for?"

"How should I know?"

"You asked me to look for it."

"For what?"

Or:

"What were we just talking about?"

"You were saying you saw Whatsisname."

"No, before that."

"I can't remember."

"Damn. Now it's gone."

And those are the better moments.

Some memory experts, of whom I have interviewed a slew, say that the problem is due mainly to the way we live: We're all on overload.

"I start going to the kitchen," a geriatric specialist tells me, "and meanwhile I'm thinking about preparing for my hospital rounds and calling the computer repair guy and dropping stuff off at the cleaner's on the way to work, and by the time I get to the kitchen, I've completely forgotten why I'm there." And this is a mere lass of forty-three.

In other words, they say, memory loss is not because we're getting older, it's simply because we have too much on our minds.

Do not believe them. It's because we're getting older.

(A cautionary note: I urge you strongly to accept this fact so that, if you should move to the country and sit moldering on the back porch, no hospital rounds, no stuff for the cleaner, no computer repair, and find that you still can't remember your neighbor's dog's name, you won't be too disappointed.)

Among my friends, who have been my friends for decades and range mostly from mid-boomer to early old age, it's the same story. We gather in a living room to watch, say, the Academy Awards — several of us insisting, as we do each year, that we watch only to see the gowns — and then somebody says, "That actress with the big lips — what's her name? I always forget her name," and somebody else says, "You're asking me?" and a third says, "I can't remember a thing anymore," and a fourth says, "Get in line," and we all laugh merrily. Much too merrily.

Because what unnerves us all, of course, is the specter of Alzheimer's disease. "My God, I must be getting Alzheimer's," we say to one another. With that same edgy little ha-ha, just to show that we are joking. More or less.

A year before I began to write this book, I found myself joking less. I had a bad case of what is not just a common phrase but a term actually used by memory researchers: tip of the tongue (TOT) syndrome.

It was not simply the obvious, such as people's names and To Do lists, that were becoming increasingly elusive but the thought process itself, sequences of thought, and as a non-fiction writer whose central task is to take a mass of research and organize it in a fluid way, moving with logic and hopefully a bit of grace from points A to B to C, I was not thrilled with this development. I would be working on a magazine article, and the perfect way to segue from one paragraph to the next would flash suddenly into my consciousness like a thousand-watt bulb, and then, *pouf,* out, gone, good-bye, and it was driving me batty.

In addition to which, often I could not see what I was writing because I could not find my eyeglasses. The title of this book, let me tell you, is a phrase carved into my soul.

And so, with a pocketful of angst, I went to see the director of a memory-aid program at a major hospital in New York City. Many big-city hospitals now have such programs. They treat primarily people with pathology, but they also get plenty of calls from people like me — those who just don't know what their memory blanks mean, and they get anxious, and they seek reassurance.

And I got it: The director put me through a battery of tests, told me that I showed no sign whatever of developing abnormal memory loss, and sent me on my way. I floated home. The old forgetfulness still drives me batty but, given the assurance that it's *normal,* I no longer lose any sleep over it. Which seems, in fact, to improve my memory.

Would that we could all relax. There is

always the possibility of being hit by dementia. Or by a truck. But the sweet *probability* is that ours is the kind of ordinary memory loss that comes with the years. It is one of the various prices of admission to longevity, and when you consider other prices that one might pay, it's the best buy in town. It even has advantages, as you will see.

Not that I am about to tout the Upside of Aging. This memory thing that we are going to explore is sometimes called benign forgetfulness. Please. Spare me the euphemisms. Less forgetfulness would be more benign. But let's recognize that, although it may drive us wild, it is totally normal — *normal:* lovable word — and move on from there.

So, although one chapter does examine why we are so preoccupied with Alzheimer's disease, and another checks out the differences between normal forgetting and signs of possible trouble, you will find no "All About Alzheimer's" in this book.

Nor will you find any other form of dementia — of which there are, by the way, some seventy different forms: seventy bitter flavors that I devoutly hope none of us ever has to taste. I know nothing much about them. But I know plenty, oh boy, about this garden-variety kind of forgetfulness that kicks in for most of us in middle age (actually it starts long before middle age, but more about that later) and leaves us hanging, mildly amused, wildly frustrated, on the cusp of some elusive fact.

Normal memory loss is what you will find in these pages. Why it happens to us, and when and how. The views (not always harmonious) of the distinguished memory specialists I have interviewed — psychiatrists, psychologists, neuroscientists, computer scientists, evolutionary biologists — all of whom are passionate on the subject of how we remember and how we forget. And the kinds of information that typically desert us first and why (Chapter One: "Say Hello to Whatisname: The Name Problem") and what to do about it; and the kinds that are almost impossible to forget and why (Chapter Six: "A Meditation on the Elephant: The Things We Never Forget").

You will also read about differences between male and female memory, some of which may be inborn and might even explain some of the differences between male and female behavior. And we will look at memory in relation to diet and diet supplements; to exercise — specifically, certain kinds of exercise — and to lifestyle; and at the shadowy business of forgetting on purpose, though not *necessarily* consciously.

Then some quirky realities: Why are we so good (alas) at remembering emotional pain but not physical pain? Why do our memories deceive us? Why will our children and our grandchildren almost certainly know more and remember less than we ever did? Why is it vital to be able *to forget?*

And then, several Big Pictures: how brain memory compares to computer memory, how forgetting is built into the great evolutionary scheme, and what the future holds in store for our memories (you can't imagine).

And, throughout, you will find the personal experiences of the many friends, colleagues, and near strangers who have been good enough to share with me moments of forgetting that they would probably rather forget. I guarantee you will recognize moments of your own among them.

I would thank them all by name, if I could only remember.

CHAPTER ONE:
SAY HELLO TO
WHATSISNAME
THE NAME PROBLEM

SCENE: Aboard a Manhattan bus, as reported in *The New York Times*

DRAMATIS PERSONAE: Two middle-aged women debating what film to see that evening.

"I want to see the movie, you know, with that woman with the long brown hair."

"Which movie is that?"

"You know, the one with that guy in it."

"The guy who was married to the singer?"

"No, the other one."

"Oh, that movie. I know the one you mean. That short, funny guy is in it."

"Right, right!"

"I heard it's not that good."

"Who said that?"

"A guy in one of the newspapers. I can't remember which one. He's also on TV."

"Oh, I know who you mean. I'm surprised. The woman you listen to on the radio loved it."

"This guy said it was tedious and too long."

"Then let's see something else. What about that movie with the plane?"

Oh, how poignantly this speaks to me. I feel as one with those women on that bus. I *am* those women on that bus.

Here am I, chasing some elusive name up and down the windowless corridors of my mind — *Yoo-hoo, name, wait for me!* — and the merry little bugger keeps outrunning me, pausing every now and again just to give me the business, make me think I can grab it, and my annoyance turns to frustration, then to indignation, then to impotent laughter — *I?* practitioner of words, fumbling around in the dark for a Tom, a Dick, a Harry? How absurd.

I begin the usual lament: "I can't remember his name, it's right here on the tip of my tongue, this is driving me crazy, you know, way back when Whatsisname was president, the Contract with America guy, *what the hell was his name?*"

Perhaps a housemate tries to be helpful, as mine does: "I think it begins with a C."

If you're lucky, he or she does not follow up, as mine once did, by waking me in the

pale light of dawn to announce triumphantly: "Newt Gingrich!" (And then the
predictable exchange: "You said it began
with a *C*." "No, I'm sure I said a *G*.")

Names, names. They are the thorn in our
communal Achilles' heel.

Question: What can you most reliably
depend upon yourself to forget?

It is the question I put to everyone I
interviewed for this book (including the
experts, most of whom are barely into
middle age, but their memories aren't what
they used to be, either).

And the lead entries were:

1. Where did I leave my glasses?
2. What was I just saying?
3. What did I come in here for?
4. What did I ask you to remind me
   to do?
5. What's her (his, its) name?

All strong contenders. But the fifth won
hands down.

There is a striking consistency to this
stuff. For almost everyone with normal
memory loss, names are the first things to
go. The genes do bless some of us with better memories than others. But, beyond the
imperatives of genes, there seems to be

27

some universal wiring system designed by master electricians of unknown origin for the precise purpose, I sometimes think, of driving us nuts.

In the sweet fullness of time, we may notice ourselves beginning to have trouble locating other sorts of words as well — common nouns, verbs, adjectives, whatever. My husband and I are both writers and work in adjacent rooms, and the SOS's ricochet back and forth.

"What is the adjective for when something is impossible to deny, when we say that it offers *blank-blank* proof?"

"Irrefutable?"

"Yes! *Irrefutable!*"

But nothing gives us more trouble than people's names. We all know it. We just don't fully understand it.

What is the logic here? Why specifically names? I wondered, as I went scurrying in hapless pursuit of them. And this was just the first of a cluster of *W* questions. As in: *Who* forgets names? Does it happen to all of us in the normal course of aging, or do some of us manage to finesse the price of admission? And *what* is actually happening that makes us forget names? (Yes, yes, we're getting older. But *what is actually happening in there?*) And *when* does it, whatever *it* is, begin to happen? And *where* is the name hiding in that maddening interval between the moment it disappears and the moment it pops out again? And *what,* if anything, can be done about it?

So, to begin: Why do we forget names?

For openers, because they don't mean anything.

Some do, obviously — June, Violet, Hill, Baker. (And some have meanings you would not suspect, such as Gloria, which, according to my trusty Webster's, is "a representation . . . of dazzling light bursting from the . . . heavens" and Betty, which is "a small instrument used by thieves in entering houses." Who knew?) But most names are words with no meaning whatever.

Which is so perverse. Again, from Webster's: "word: a speech sound . . . that symbolizes and communicates a meaning . . ." But it is the idiosyncratic nature of those particular words we call proper names that they defy Webster. Your name refers to nothing except you — and anyone else who may have the same name, which only complicates matters. It has no context. It does not belong to any category of meaning; it does not provide a tie or a clue to anything — except to you.

In short, it totally fails to do what *lamp-*

shade and *shoe* and *farmhouse* do plenty of: trigger an association. Which is a crucial failing, because that is how memory works: by association.

Ah, but wait: If names give us trouble essentially because they are meaningless, they were just as meaningless when we were children, and they never gave us any trouble back then. Why now?

Which brings us to the next *W*: *What* is actually happening as we age that creates this trifling, maddening problem?

Actually, three things are happening.

Dr. Norman Relkin, a neurologist and neuroscientist, is the director of the Weill Cornell Memory Disorders Program at New York-Presbyterian Hospital in Manhattan. He says: "People ask me 'Why is it that I used to remember names when I went to a cocktail party, and now I can't?' "

And then he explains: Just as names begin giving us grief, two other extremely common problems are kicking in. It is becoming harder to do several things at once, otherwise known as multitasking, and it is taking us longer to process new information.

Thus, Dr. Relkin says, "If you combine the primary decline in naming ability with a decreased ability to multitask, to take in everything that's going on at once at a cocktail party, *plus* a slowing of reaction time, you can see . . ."

Yes. I certainly can.

Now, as to the *who* of it: Do we all eventually, inevitably, experience the name problem?

Answer: Not all but almost. Some rare birds do wing through life, even into *old* old age (defined by social scientists as ninety plus), with their memory systems totally intact. What explains them?

It is a hot question in memory research now. Maybe those lucky few always ate right, slept plenty, exercised the body, activated the mind — all the things that we are urged to do to improve our memories. (Chess has become a chic recommendation; crossword puzzles, too. Not everyone agrees, as you'll see in Chapter Five. All we know for sure is that they can't hurt, unless you use them, as I often do, to avoid doing whatever it is that you ought to be doing instead.)

Most studies do suggest that all of the above help, but the likelihood is that people with superior memories always had superior memories. Probably they could stay up half the night, scarfing down pizza and watching old Charlie Chan movies, and *still* have superior memories. Genes, genes.

One theory being floated about among cognitive scientists is that education may also make a difference — that people who have more education may learn to solve problems in more efficient ways than those with less, which may actually, physiologically, modify the way their brains work. I happen to know plenty of PhD's whose memories are even worse than my own, but that is off the point. The point being, if you are well into middle age (generally defined as the stretch between forty-five and sixty-five) with no hint whatever of the name problem, here's to you, kid. You are a rare bird indeed.

Next, then: *When,* on average, does all this begin?

This one is a thunderbolt, at least for me, from Dr. Relkin: "If you control for education, for socioeconomic status, for all the other variables that might influence this, *after, really, the twenties, you start to see some loss of primary memory function.*" (Italics mine.) "It's something which I think is grounded, now, in the biology of the brain."

New technology, he says, has given cognitive researchers the ability to measure changes in the brain over time. "And with it, we can see that, in the general population, people's brains shrink by about one-half of one percent per year."

"From what age on?"

"In the studies that I've seen, beginning in the thirties."

In the thirties! Whether this should make us feel better or worse, I'm not sure. But it does suggest a snappy comeback if your children ever heckle you, however tenderly, about your memory.

The name problem does not become big enough to start systematically bugging us until pretty well along in middle age. But when it does start: *Where* are the little devils hiding when we can't find them?

I get the answer to this one from Dr. Yaakov Stern, the head of a team of scientists who do research on aging and memory at the Columbia University College of Physicians and Surgeons in New York City.

Dr. Stern is a neuropsychologist. His particular interest is in people whose memories remain intact throughout their lifetimes. Like everyone I have met who toils in these fields, he seems to be totally in love with his subject. He is very affable and very tall, and, as he answers my questions, his upper body seems to bend forward, like the body of one of those improbably long-legged birds, with the weight of his enthusiasm.

"One part of the brain has to do with storing memory, let's say, and another part has to do with retrieving it," he says. "The hippocampus and areas around it seem to be very important for putting new memories in, and certain areas in the front of the brain are important for retrieving. It's almost like the World Wide Web — there's a lot of information sitting in there but you need the right search function to pull it out.

"Remembering names is very different from what we call *semantic memory:* what a desk is, what a chair is, what animals versus furniture are. All that stuff is ingrained in a very different way from a fact such as your name. But names you grow up with — like the name of my father, say — such names become so ingrained that they may be stored like semantic memory."

Which does not explain my Brad Pitt/Tom Cruise syndrome: "What about when I'm watching a movie and I say, 'Now, I've seen that actor a hundred times and I still can't remember his name.' It may not be a name I grew up with, but it's certainly familiar. Why can't I come up with it?"

"And an hour later, you're standing in the shower, and, *boom!* the name comes to you. Right?"

"*Boom!* Right." On good days.

"So it's *in there.* That's the retrieval problem — that's when you need the search function."

And where is it when we need it? Ah, there's the final rub.

Not to burden any of us with technical detail — we have quite enough to forget as is — but current thinking among neuroscientists is that the brain's frontal lobe, which is involved in the search function, is one of the first areas that start to shrink as we age. Which is *normal,* friends. "So it may not be the ability to store memories but the ability to retrieve them that is affected with aging."

So when we are trying to pull out a name, the poor maligned object is not willfully hiding there in the fuzzy depths of the brain. It is simply having trouble finding its way out. Patience. That frontal lobe may need time to boot up.

What, then, can be done about it?

Compensatory strategies: that's the operative phrase. The experts all stress that no strategy can recover what has been lost. If my frontal lobe has shrunk, it's shrunk. But we can compensate for our weaknesses by playing to our strengths.

The commercial woods are full of self-styled memory gurus who promise the moon. They run clinics, publish books, produce audiovisual cassettes, advertise widely and sensationally ("I can give you a photographic memory in just two hours! Pay only . . ."). Simply master their techniques and practice, practice, practice, and you will "have a memory like a magnet," "achieve the fame and financial freedom you deserve," "entertain your guests and be the life of the party" — a prospect that's enough to send me running in the opposite direction — and never forget another name as long as you live.

It's like all those perennial how to's: How to Get Thin and Stay Thin, How to Keep Married Sex Hot, How to Make a Million in Real Estate. Memory is big, big business.

They all teach basically the same strategies, most of which are variations on strategies that are at least a couple of thousand years old, having been invented by the *real* gurus: the ancient Romans. They use elaborate word associations and visual imagery (*mnemonics,* in the trade; a verbal clue is a mnemonic, so is a string tied around the finger, so is any device that may help you remember). Woody Allen needled them slyly in the 2006 movie *Scoop.* "I have a mnemonic system," his character says. "Say I want to remember this ashtray. I think of fifty ashtrays dancing in miniskirts."

In my experience, most of those touted strategies are just too complicated to be useful. We do not need to be given complexities to memorize for the purpose of helping our memories. What we need is simplicity.

The programs affiliated with hospitals usually recommend simple devices for remembering names, three of them so basic that you've probably used them intuitively. They are *phonemic cueing,* which is cueing by sound or by letter; *semantic cueing,* which is cueing by context; and what psychologists call *spaced rehearsal technique,* which works by repetition.

Whenever you say, "I think it sounds like . . ." or "I think it begins with . . . ," that's phonemic cueing. It is one of the elegant little mysteries of the mind that you sometimes can dredge up the right initial but not the name — or the wrong initial leads you down the right path, as in my husband's "I think it begins with a C . . . Newt Gingrich!"

Frequently I find myself marching through the alphabet in search of a clue: Andrew,

Bob, Carol, Donna, Ed . . . which is nice when you hit the jackpot but deeply boring. And it doesn't help me hit the jackpot all that often, though it may work nicely for you.

Perhaps the simplest strategy is spaced rehearsal technique, which is just a fancy phrase for repeating something again and again, but over time. *Spaced* is the operative word. Rapid cramming — muttering someone's name to yourself over and over in rapid succession — is not the best way to commit a name (or anything else) to memory. Far better to repeat it silently when you first hear it, wait ten seconds, silently say it again, wait twenty seconds, bring it back up, wait thirty seconds, repeat . . .

It is easy to get into the habit of doing this, and I find it's pretty effective. On a scale of one to ten, I'd give it a seven.

Semantic cueing is a bit more involved but not much. Since memory is helped by context, and names have none, the idea here is to supply one. As in this scenario from Cornell's Dr. Relkin: "You may remember that you met so-and-so (whose name you can't remember) at the zoo. And you start thinking, 'Was it at the giraffe exhibition? At the monkey cage? Who else was with me that day?' . . . And since the mind and memory work by association, by bringing up related items, it sometimes greases the wheels of recall." Sometimes, yes, it has greased the wheels for me.

Association of this kind is a form of *elaboration,* which simply means taking what you already know and linking it in some way to what you want to remember — in this case, a name.

An example: If the name is Jane, you might establish a link by thinking of her in relation to some other Jane you have known: how you feel about that other Jane or how this one seems in some particular feature — the voice, the coloring, the body shape — similar to, or strikingly different from, that other one. Or you could link her to Janes you have *not* known: Jane Fonda, Jane Eyre, Lady Jane Grey, "You Tarzan, me Jane" . . . Or, if this Jane happens to have great hair, or if you happen not to be enchanted by her, you might make a rhyme: "Jane has a mane," or "Jane is a pain." Although, of course, if Jane is a pain, why should you knock yourself out remembering her name?

Anyway, this is the one that works best for me. I'd give it a nine. (Nothing is perfect.) It is not for no reason that, just as real estate specialists keep reciting the mantra "location, location, location," memory specialists keep reciting the mantra "elaboration, elaboration, elaboration."

Linking the name to visual imagery can work very well, as long as you keep it simple. In the technique commonly taught by the heavy-hype gurus, it is not so simple. You are instructed to find words that can be put together to sound like the name you want to remember, then to use them to create strange mental images — the stranger the better, because strange is memorable.

Example: You meet John Doe. You might transpose *John* into the mental picture of a bathroom — its tiled walls, its mirror, its sink — and *Doe* into the image of a deer standing at that sink and looking in the mirror. The name Mary Smith might be visualized as a woman who is dressed in full bridal regalia (*Mary/marry*) and wielding a blacksmith's hammer.

This technique can become so convoluted it pretzels the brain. One guru I interviewed suggested how to render my own name unforgettable (to others; I tend to remember it): For Martha, he said, visualize a *Martian,* preferably green; for Weinman, see a tiny *man* encased in a gigantic *wine* bottle; for Lear, see that tiny man with a *leer* on his face, a big lascivious grin. Now put them all together and you've got a green Martian staring at a miniature man in a gigantic wine bottle who is . . . *Enough,* I thought. Get me and that poor little bastard in the wine bottle out of here.

Remember, you've got to come up with this kind of thing *quickly,* upon being introduced to Whatsisname. Neat trick. Is it possible to learn? Sure. It is also possible to learn Greek.

But when it is kept simple, visualization is an enormously effective mnemonic, because mental images have relative staying power. Most of us retain good visual memory long after our verbal memory has started going a little flabby. Which is to say, you are likely to remember what Whatsisname looks like long after you have forgotten his name.

In crowded social settings, the "Quick, what's his name?" anxiety level may rise sharply, which almost guarantees that you won't remember anything — an excess of nervous adrenaline is flooding the roadways. When this happens, and mnemonics cannot help, I heartily recommend using the dodges that most of us develop to cover our tracks. They are, after all, only mildly dissembling.

Dr. Stern, who says, as many of us do, that he was *never* too good with names, describes his own method: "I'm talking to someone and a third person comes up and

I know I have to introduce them but I can't remember their names. So I say, 'Do you two know each other?' And then I just hope they'll go ahead and do the introductions themselves. Which, thank heaven, they usually do."

I am more devious. The room is crowded, the sound level is deafening, and I am having a conversation, or trying to have a conversation, with X (whose name, of course, escapes me) when Y (ditto) joins us. What to do?

Answer: Nothing. I greet Y and keep talking. If neither of them asks for an introduction, there's no problem. If either says, "I don't think we've met," I say, on a note of high surprise, "Oh, I was *sure* you two knew each other!" Pregnant pause, which they either do, or do not, fill in with their names. If they do, I am home free. If they don't, I say, "Sorry, I'll be right back" and head for the bathroom, the cloakroom, the bar, anywhere but there.

Now, however, I cannot rely on elaboration or semantic cueing or spaced rehearsal technique, all rendered useless because I don't remember the damn names. You can see the problem. So I am left with phonetics: Karen, Larry, Molly, Nancy . . .

Which may work or not. Generally not.

But by the time I've gone through the alphabet, those two guests whose names I didn't remember will either have done the honors for themselves or moved along to other guests whose names, let me assure you, I will not remember.

Why fret? So I've blanked on your name and you've blanked on mine and none of the usual mnemonics are working at all. We still have a lulu in reserve and it is, for my money, the best, the easiest, the most efficient mnemonic of them all:

"I'm *so* sorry, but I've forgotten your name. Would you mind telling it to me again?"

Foolproof. And nobody will ever hate you for wanting to remember who they are.

Chapter Two:
Multitasking,
Anyone?

THE ATTENTION PROBLEM

"Sweetheart," she says, "when you walk the dog, will you mail this letter for me?"

"Okay."

"And pick up my dress from the cleaner's?"

"Okay."

"And you know what I'm really dying for? A hot fudge sundae with vanilla ice cream and nuts and a cherry on top."

"Okay." He heads for the door.

"Wait! Write it down or you'll forget."

"I won't forget. Hot fudge sundae, vanilla ice cream, nuts, and a cherry on top." He exits.

Soon he returns, carrying a small paper bag.

Inside reposes a bagel.

"I told you!" she says. "You forgot the cream cheese."

In truth, I have been forgetting the cream cheese all my life.

This process we call multitasking has never been my strong suit. I have been forever doing seven things at once and finishing none of them. But in recent years this tendency keeps getting worse, which gives heft to my theory that we really do not change much as we get older, not in any fundamental way. We simply become more of whatever we were to begin with.

This theory is based on a broad foundation of no scientific testing whatever. Nonetheless. Look around. Proof abounds.

Well, then. A typical morning, quite recent: I am getting laundry ready for the cleaning woman who comes on Mondays. I always do a little tidying in advance so that she will not find out what a domestic disaster I am.

While sorting linens, I notice a ripped seam. Minor, easily fixable. I go to the sewing box, find a long-missing button for a winter coat, get out the coat, which reminds me that I still haven't stored my woolens for the summer, so I open a sweater drawer and begin brushing sweaters, which instantly reminds me that someone (who? I think it begins with a *B*) said that whole cloves are a better moth repellent than mothballs, so I head for the kitchen spice rack, at which point the telephone rings.

When the call ends, there is the trail of detritus, laundry room to linen closet to coat closet to sweater drawer to kitchen to telephone, and not a single task has been completed.

I can't put it all down to overload. We are all on overload. But so were our great-grandparents — mine, anyway — who had to gather the wood to stoke the fire to heat the water to wash the clothes and so forth, and God knows what they did about storing the woolens.

And I can't blame only my own untidy nature. No, this is a thing that begins to happen to most of us in the fine fullness of our middle years, and doubtless happened to our forebears, too: We start finding it harder to divide our attention, otherwise and odiously known as multitasking. (A brief aside: There are certain words and phrases that drive me bonkers. I can't say why. "Quality time" is one, "growing the economy" is another, and "multitasking" is right up there.)

Anyway, whatever you call it, it is the second of the three most common symptoms of normal memory loss, almost on a par with forgetting names. And kicking in at the same time — ah, the timing of the gods — is the third of this troika: processing. It starts taking us longer to process new information. Both of these are far greater problems for us than they were for those forebears, because so many of us are still working full-time, with all the attendant pressures, at ages when they had long since been put, or put themselves, out to pasture.

Memory experts recite as catechism that familiar holy quartet of factors that affect memory:

1. Eating healthily
2. Avoiding stress (tee-hee)
3. Getting lots of sleep
4. Getting regular exercise, including mental exercise

We all do know, or should know, plenty about the holy quartet. It is hard to live in this time and this place and *not* know what constitutes a good diet, a good exercise regimen, management of stress, and the importance of all these to good memory. But when it comes to understanding the normal *bad* memory (which only *sounds* like an oxymoron) that may hit us because of trouble multitasking and slowing of reaction time, we don't know much.

One cause of these problems seems to lie in the hippocampus, the area of the brain that is considered a kind of receiving and distribution center for new information. The Memory Place — that is what it is called by Dr. Margaret Sewell, the director of the Memory Enhancement Program at Mount Sinai Hospital in New York City.

"Any damage in the hippocampal area is going to result in memory problems of one sort or another," she says. "And starting in your mid-forties, probably, you lose cells from that area at a rather significant rate. This is normal." (It is also normal to be *gaining* cells in that area; the hippocampus is now believed to generate new cells throughout our lifetimes, though the process slows with age.) "As in most cases, we can understand pathology better than normal functioning. A considerable amount is understood about Alzheimer's disease — what is going wrong. But when things are going right, we understand less."

It is the usual irony. Normal is not sexy. Normal does not attract the pharmaceutical giants and press coverage. Normal does not create (à la cancer or AIDS or, for that matter, Alzheimer's) the special interest groups and the lobbies and the public outcries for causes and cures.

Dr. Sewell is vibrant and full of Boston Irish charm and looks like a girl. She was forty-two when we met and already feeling the pinch, as I learned when I asked if she'd seen any change in her own memory function.

"Oh, yes. Trouble finding the right word. Much more trouble multitasking, relative to my twenties — that is *so* hard for me now. All that has been happening since my twenties, but people don't usually notice it until they get to their forties."

Blessedly, the multitask problem is much easier to treat than to understand. Here is how Dr. Sewell and her colleagues approach it in the Mount Sinai program. "Let me say first, this isn't about being able to go on *Oprah* and recite five thousand digits. What we aim for is not so much improvement of skills as compensating for skills that may be declining. We know that that's true of our physical lives: Whether you're eighteen or fifty-eight, you can run the marathon, but the way you train for it will be very different. If I'm fifty-eight, I've got to start out walking, then I've got to run a quarter mile, then I've got to compensate and take the aspirin ahead of time . . . The same thing is true of cognition. Yet we have this myth that it should be just like it was at eighteen."

I ask, "You're suggesting that just as we accept that our physical capacities will change, we should accept that our cognitive capacities will change, too?"

"Absolutely!" (She would get a fight from researchers who argue that the problem is not age but lifestyle. Like most memory specialists, Dr. Sewell blames both and, Lord knows, there is plenty of blame to go around.) "Because once you accept it, you can begin to compensate for the changes and make a difference in your daily life.

"In the typical work environment, we do everything wrong. I have e-mail, a phone, a fax, a pager; the secretary is talking to me; I'm on the cell phone; and I'm also trying to read an article that I have to give a lecture on in an hour. And I'm saying, 'Hm, how come I'm not remembering much from this article?'

"The way to compensate for that is simple: I change the way I organize my tasks. I say: 'For the next twenty minutes, no calls and no e-mail.' You know that sign that you have e-mail, and the temptation to see what it is? All that is *off* for these twenty minutes that I'll spend reading this article before I have to lecture. I will save certain tasks for certain times of day. I won't try to plan a vacation while the TV is on and the phone is ringing. It's not rocket science, but it is *amazing* the difference that people notice as they begin to cut down on any multitasking they don't absolutely have to do. But we're so fast in our culture; people just don't tend to try it."

It is not *too* wild an oversimplification to think of the memory process as a drama in three acts:

1. Acquisition — taking in a new item of information
2. Storage — filing it away
3. Retrieval — pulling it out

When we complain that we have forgotten something, what we usually mean — as both Dr. Sewell and Columbia University's Dr. Stern say — is that we can't retrieve it: I can't find this thing that's in my head somewhere. But if we weren't paying attention when we heard it, it may never have gotten stored. And what is not stored obviously cannot be retrieved.

"The key to healthy memory functioning at *any* age is attention," Dr. Sewell says. "Everything you need to do to improve memory revolves around that ability: to pay attention. So you accept that you can't read the entire morning paper on the train to work while a fight is going on in the train and music is blasting and you're listening to your own music on your earphones. You get to the office and there's a crisis at work and then you think, 'My God, my memory is going. I don't remember a *thing* that I read this morning.'

"Well, how could you possibly? I mean, an eighteen-year-old might be able to pull it off. An eighteen-year-old can study for a chemistry test in the middle of a keg party in college and still pass. But as you get older, you have to pick and choose. Be *brutal* about it."

(That same eighteen-year-old may well be ramping up his attentional capacity with amphetamines. It is well established that such stimulants as amphetamine, caffeine, and nicotine may improve one's concentration. I can attest to it. I was for three decades the heaviest smoker I knew: two to two and a half packs a day, every day, only excepting bouts of flu and fever. Repeatedly I tried to quit and always lost the battle at the typewriter, where I could not concentrate on the work or on anything else except on wanting, desperately, a cigarette. What finally did the trick was none of the health threats, the descriptions of emphysema, or pictures of cancer-ridden lungs with which they tried to wean me off the wretched weed in clinics at the American Heart Association, the American Cancer Society, and the Seventh-day Adventists (nor a visit to a hypnotist), but rather the creeping sense that I was becoming more and more a social pariah. Then I quit for good and thought I would die for lack of the ability to concentrate. That lasted for several difficult months. A big help, by the way, at least for me: nicotine gum.

Now, twenty years later, the mere odor of cigarette smoke breaks into my concentration and makes me feel queasy. So much for the indispensability of stimulants.)

I reviewed Dr. Sewell's approach with two friends who are almost as lacking in self-discipline as I. And we all gave it a try — not *brutal,* perhaps, but resolute — and we have all had essentially the same result.

We still find it hard to finish one stray task before hopping on to another. But when it comes to *categories* of tasks — such as not reading e-mail until a certain hour, not answering non-emergency telephone calls until a certain amount of work is done, not going on any errands until the bills are paid — by imposing rigid sequence upon such daily tasks, we have found that, rocket science or no, it does clean up our acts. Dramatically.

In recent years, as multitasking has started

to become more of a problem, I myself have patched together various little mnemonic devices, all of them extremely simple, all based on linking and associating — the kind of thing that many of us arrive at intuitively — that work well for me.

I am a big fan of acronyms. If I have to pick up my shoes at the shoe repair shop tomorrow, go to the optometrist to have my eyeglasses fixed, and remember to buy some butter, I will pluck out *B* for *butter, O* for *optometrist, S* for *shoe* repair: BOSS. In the morning, there it is, oh yes: BOSS. Go do it.

Or I use the reliable old mental-image technique. I visualize the route I will follow from my home to the cobbler to the optometrist to the supermarket, really *seeing* that route in my mind's eye.

Or I create a little narrative, nothing fancy: Tomorrow I have to get my eyeglasses fixed so that I can read the "sell before" date on the butter and make sure that the shoes look properly repaired.

Whatever works. But if the list of tasks is long, I don't even try any of the above. Why knock myself out? I make a written list. That's what written lists are for.

The third of that troika of memory problems, the slowing of ability to absorb new information, is equally improvable.

What we must do, Dr. Sewell says, is be more generous to ourselves — never painful advice to follow. We must give ourselves more time for absorption and elaboration.

In a memory test that she describes, a story is read, just once, to a group of people who are in their twenties and in their seventies. Half an hour later, they are asked individually how much of the story they can remember. The young people always do better.

"And the older ones always say, 'Does that mean that my memory is getting worse?' Well, some research suggests that it's not memory per se that declines, as much as cognitive processing speed. The older people simply need more exposure to the material. Give them *three* trials of that story, back to back, and half an hour later the seventy-five-year-old may remember it just as well as the twenty-five-year-old."

The implications are lovely: "If you're willing to concentrate a little bit harder, to pare down your distractions, to rehearse more, practice more . . . You say you want to learn Italian when you're ninety? Okay! It is going to take you a little longer, but, assuming that there's no pathology, you can do it!"

Extremely bright, high-achieving people who have jobs in which they must remember a great deal, and on several fronts at once, often come to her office *freaked out,* Dr. Sewell says, because they are functioning less efficiently than they used to. They ask her, "How come I can't remember a novel that I read on the beach last summer, but I can remember soliloquies from *Hamlet* that I read in the tenth grade?"

Leaving aside that I feel deeply grateful not to remember the novels that I read on the beach last summer, this connects to a question I have often asked myself: How is it that I cannot remember a single line of dialogue from a movie that I saw last week, but I can remember to perfection the lyrics to "My Funny Valentine" and "My Way" and "These Foolish Things Remind Me of You"?

Answer: rehearsal and elaboration.

Those of us who studied *Hamlet* did not simply read it. We discussed it scene by scene, we probably had to memorize "To be or not to be . . . ," and to practice it at home, recite it aloud in class, dissect it line by line, write a paper about it, be tested on it.

In short, we had vastly more rehearsal of

that material than we did of a pop novel that we read in a couple of hours last summer. And Lord knows how many times in a lifetime I have listened to, and sung, my Sinatra favorites. Absorption time? Long enough to have been absorbed right into my bones.

Absorption time. Here is a workaday example from Dr. Sewell:

Have trouble keeping up with the news? Have limited time to do it?

Don't try to read the entire paper. Instead, concentrate on the front-page stories. Maybe even try reading just the headlines and first paragraphs. Read them several times, ask yourself questions about them:

What was the main word in the headline?
What was the gist of this paragraph?
What were the three major points it made?

And so forth, just as if you were being tested back in high school.

I tried it. Minor investment, big return. It took me far less time to absorb far more information, and it stayed longer.

The historian Ronald Chernow, fifty-eight, who has written award-winning, epic-length biographies of Alexander Hamilton, J. P. Morgan, and John D. Rockefeller, Sr., has to perform herculean feats of memory with each book. He describes to me how he uses the concept of absorption time:

"A big memory trick for me is to think of it as a two-step process. First, my mind takes something in. But that will fade fast unless I reinforce it. So then I make notes on it." (N.B.: He makes those notes on four-by-six index cards. Twenty to thirty thousand index cards. Per book.) "Or I go for a walk and keep reviewing it, and then make notes. There has to be that second step to fix it, really *fix* it, in my memory.

"Long ago, I took something called the Evelyn Wood Speed Reading Course. The method they taught was to move your finger back and forth across a page, and then to jot down what you retained. I thought it was all bogus. But then I realized that they had had this insight of taking the second step. People remembered more and credited the method. But really, it was because they were making those notes."

Dr. Sewell says that her own father is a dramatic example of what can be accomplished when we give ourselves the time to take in new material. He is in his late sixties, working in a business that involves the physics of software.

"He goes to seminars with these kids —

he calls them kids; they're in their thirties — where they have to absorb a huge amount of new and complex information. And he panics because he just can't take it in that fast, and they come back the next day and the kids have it all in their heads. He's sure he is getting Alzheimer's.

"Well, I don't think he is getting Alzheimer's at all. He's found — partly from my talking with him, I suppose — that if he goes home with a manual and spends some time over the weekend organizing the information in his head, by Monday morning he's up to speed with the thirty-five-year-olds.

"Many people simply do not realize that they can compensate for these things. You have to become an active learner. You have to take the information in through different senses — meaning that you don't just read something, you take notes, you ask questions, you write it all down, you say it out loud. And then you say it out loud again."

Just as with that *Hamlet* soliloquy.

Or with *these foolish things* that *remind me of yoooou* . . .

Ah, poetry of my young heart. I'll forget my own name before I forget those lyrics.

So when I need to memorize, I do as

advised: I take time, I take notes, I rehearse, I recite, I aim to be an active learner. All fine compensatory tactics.

But when it's multiple-task time — which means for many of us the innumcrable and often overlapping daily tasks of work life, home life, and social life — I don't believe in driving my brain parts crazy with challenge. I revert to my all-purpose, all-weather, all-time favorite compensatory tactic: Lists. *Lists,* my fellow toiling multi-taskers.

Consider this: Have the maestros of memory, the keenest minds working at the greatest research centers in the world, ever come up with anything better than the list titled Things to Do Tomorrow?

Never.

All I need to remember is where I put the list.

> "The horror of that moment," the King went on, "I shall never, *never* forget."
> "You will, though," the Queen said, "if you don't make a memorandum of it."
> — Lewis Carroll, *Through the Looking-Glass*

CHAPTER THREE: LOSE SOME, WIN SOME

THE UPSIDE OF FORGETTING

Imagine, if you can, Sherlock Holmes, the immortal maestro of memory, preaching the virtues of forgetfulness.

Holmes, who can tell what brand you smoke (as I, with the passion of an ex-smoker, hope you do not) simply by smelling the ash, and where you have traveled by eyeing the dust on your shoe. Holmes, who is blessed, as he himself would be happy to tell you, by the best memory, the sharpest perception, the greatest gift for total recall this side of the Thames — it is this Holmes, of all people, who lectures us on, of all subjects, the importance of forgetting.

Well, *no problem,* maestro. You're talking to experts.

His lecture comes in *A Study in Scarlet,* the very first Sherlock Holmes mystery. Here's the setup:

Holmes and Dr. Watson have just met. They are both young, both extremely short on cash, and for economy's sake have agreed to share a flat — the famous digs at No. 221B Baker Street.

As they become acquainted, Watson starts discovering some weird gaps in his room-mate's astonishing array of knowledge, and none weirder than this: Holmes does not know that the earth revolves around the sun.

Watson can't believe it. He is stunned. As he himself tells us:

"You appear to be astonished," he said, smiling at my expression of surprise. "Now that I do know it, I shall do my best to forget it."

"To forget it!"

"You see," he explained, "I consider that a man's brain originally is like a little empty attic, and you have to stock it with such furniture as you choose. A fool takes in all the lumber of every sort that he comes across, so that the knowledge which might be useful to him gets crowded out, or at best is jumbled up with a lot of other things, so that he has a difficulty in laying his hands upon it. Now the skilful work-man is very careful indeed as to what he takes into his brain-attic. He will have noth-ing but the tools which may help him in doing his work, but of these he has a large assortment, and all in the most perfect order. It is a mistake to think that that little room has elastic walls and can distend to any extent. Depend upon it there comes a time when for every addition of knowledge you forget something that you knew before. It is of the highest importance, therefore, not to have useless facts elbowing out the useful ones."

"But the Solar System!" I protested.

"What the deuce is it to me?" he interrupted impatiently: "you say that we go round the sun. If we went round the moon it would not make a pennyworth of difference to me or to my work."

Now that's what I call self-confidence.

Cunning idea, that the mind operates like a revolving-door system — a fact comes in, a fact goes out. Cunning but untrue.

We may pound our heads and say, "The disk is full" or "There's no more room on the hard drive." (Just as our parents said "I must be getting old" — pretty much the same sentiment, but who says *that* anymore? Amid the imperatives of political correctness, *deaf* is *hearing challenged, retarded* is *exceptional,* and *old* does not exist.) But we don't really know how expandable the walls of that brain-attic may be.

It is true, as the neurologist Dr. Barry Gordon, founder of the Memory Clinic at Johns Hopkins in Baltimore, has said: "When people get older, there is more interference from other memories. There's a pile of material in your head that younger people don't have."

A mixed blessing, as he points out: It takes longer to dig out what you know because you know so much more than you used to. But there is no evidence whatever that a whit of that knowledge must be junked to make space for more knowledge.

Holmes is dead right, though, on his central point: Forgetting is essential. This sounds as counterintuitive as that immortal movie line delivered by the actor Michael Douglas: "Greed is good." But it is true: Forgetting is indispensable. Forgetting, I will say at risk of sounding too sentimental, is part of what makes us human — which is why many memory experts believe that we are actually, biologically, programmed to forget.

I am in the office of Dr. Gayatri Devi, a clinical associate professor of neurology and psychiatry at the New York University School of Medicine and director of the New York Memory Services, who specializes in treating memory disorders. This office, in which innumerable clients have expressed their fears — often misplaced — that something unfrivolously funny was happening to their memory, looks like a comfy upscale living room. A big beautiful dog is snoring blissfully on the floor. (Dr. Devi is also beautiful, a fact I note because neurologist/psychiatrists are not, as a breed, lookers.)

The doctor is explaining that process whereby we are forever screening, selecting, filtering input, making decisions about what we will remember and what we will not — and doing it without a conscious thought.

"The thing that people forget," she says pithily, "is that we are *meant* to forget. Why? Well, because the primary function of an organism is always to survive. And if I can't forget in this minute all the things in this room around me, if I can't forget what's on the walls, what's on the floor" (The dog — can she forget the dog?) "if I can't forget how everything here looks and feels, if I can't prioritize what I need to remember, then I'm taken up with all kinds of extraneous details, I can't attend to you, I'm not able to connect, and I fail as an organism."

We know very well how to forget on purpose. Perhaps unconsciously, but on purpose nonetheless. For example: We forget invitations that we somehow felt trapped into accepting. (A good rule here is never to accept any invitation that you don't want to reciprocate. I don't always obey it, but it's a good rule.) We forget to telephone people because we are angry at them, or because they didn't remember to telephone us, or because who knows why.

Many studies have shown that when we are feeling depressed, we have great trouble remembering any of the happy times in our lives, though we have a remarkably good memory for the unhappy times. The memory feeds on the emotion and the emotion on the memory, and round and round we go. Downhill.

We are more apt to forget the names of people we dislike than of people we like. I think of a friend who suddenly blanked out on the name of her ex-husband, to whom she had been married for eleven years. "Can you *believe* it?" she said. Of course I can. The mind, after all, has a mind of its own. Memory has bias. She hated that man; his name was buried under so many compacted layers of hate, small wonder she couldn't dig it out.

Forgetting names is also a time-honored and not *necessarily* conscious form of one-upmanship. (The world turns, but human nature does not. "We may with advantage at times forget what we know," the Syrian writer Publilius Syrus said. He said it in 42 B.C.)

But none of this is what Holmes had in mind. He was talking about the need to steer a path through the sludge of information that assaults us every day, which he does so much more cagily than we.

Think of those staged events that are a staple of law school classes: Someone charges into the room, pulls out a gun, shoots someone else, and there is a great deal of yelling and falling down and carrying on, and then the class comes to order and everyone is asked what happened.

There will be such dramatically different recollections (eyewitness accounts, we call them!) as to drive a jury crazy, because we do not really perceive — we only think we do — everything that's going on.

Conan Doyle's man, of course, would miss only the irrelevant details. Which is the crucial difference between Holmes and us: The maestro forgets by design. We do it on automatic. But we also do, despite ourselves, a great deal of efficient forgetting. And a good thing it is, too.

The Cornell University neurologist Norman Relkin minces no words: *Forgetting is almost as important as remembering.*" (Italics mine.) "We have to be able to forget things which are not salient, because if we did not, we would be in a perpetual state of information overload." A state in which we would be in big, big trouble.

There are conditions in which people do lose the ability to forget. They are called, in fact, disorders of forgetting.

The most familiar one, heartbreakingly familiar in times of war, is post-traumatic stress disorder: The victims of traumatic events, such as fires, rapes, violent accidents, natural disasters, are unable to escape their memories (except, perhaps, through chemical intervention, a highly controversial prospect that we will explore in Chapter Seventeen, "Beyond the Botox Generation: Memory and Tomorrow").

We've seen those war movies about trauma endlessly relived — he's on the battlefield, shells exploding all around him, sees his buddy blown apart, comes home, freaks out every time a door bangs behind him — we've seen enough of those to recognize the syndrome, even when we do not have the real thing to remind us.

But there are less familiar disorders of forgetting. There is a famous case in literature, a short story called "Funes, the Memorious" by the Argentinean writer Jorge Luis Borges.

Funes, a village innocent, is thrown by a horse and knocked out. When he regains consciousness, he finds that he has become a memory machine. The accident, which has left him crippled, has also left him with perfect memory. He remembers everything. And he can forget nothing.

He has total recall of every single thing that has ever happened to him, every fact he has ever learned, every person he has ever met, every word ever spoken to him or by him, every detail of every sight ("every leaf of every tree," Borges writes) that has ever come within his line of vision.

Further, it is what professionals call *eidetic memory,* meaning visual memory, and what the rest of us commonly call photographic memory. Each memory sits in Funes's beleaguered brain as a distinct mental image. He cannot think, he cannot sleep; all he can do is remember. He is immobilized by the burden of his memories. "My memory, sir, is like a garbage heap," he tells the narrator.

Borges himself said that the story was no more than a long metaphor for insomnia. But reading it, I thought of the real-life case of a man whose fate sounded much like that of the hapless Funes. They are, in fact, astoundingly alike, except that one is a fictional creation and the other is one of the most renowned case studies in the history of memory research.

The Russian psychologist Aleksandr Romanovich Luria, professor of psychology at the University of Moscow, spent twenty years studying his subject, whom he identified simply as S. (later known to be Shereshevskii). In 1968, he reported his findings in a book called *The Mind of a Mnemonist,* subtitled *A Little Book About a Vast Memory.*

Vast, indeed. S.'s potential for memory was beyond measure. Literally. Scientists could not measure it. Those brain-attic walls of Conan Doyle's imagining were simply blown wide open.

"I had been unable," Dr. Luria tells us, "to perform what one would think would be the simplest task a psychologist can do: measure the capacity of an individual's memory . . . for it appeared that there was no limit either to the capacity of S.'s memory or to the durability of the traces he retained."

What psychologists call *short-term memory* is typically gone after seconds, as opposed to *long-term memory,* which is the kind that goes into deep storage. A common example: You look up a telephone number in the directory, you keep repeating it as you move to the telephone, you punch in the number, you get a busy signal. You hang up. A minute or two later, when you're ready to try it again, you have to look it up again. That's short-term memory.

For S., short-term memory did not exist. Everything was long-term. Luria gave him a series of words or numbers — thirty, fifty, seventy at a time — and he recited back the series in perfect order. When Luria retested him years later, *fifteen years* later, by which time S. had become a famous mnemonist, performing Olympic-scale feats of memory onstage, he could still recite, flawlessly, any of those series.

The workings of such minds are a mystery. Probably the people who own them are wired a bit differently than the rest of us. They have innately superior memories that may be further sharpened by using elaborate mnemonic devices, substituting numbers for letters and creating bizarre visual images, as described in Chapter One — techniques that are easy for them to master, though not for us.

People with such memories may end up, as S. did, performing onstage. They will invite, say, a hundred members of the audience to call out their names and then repeat the names in perfect sequence, to everyone's amazement. Eidetic memory can be a blessing, or at least a cash cow. But it can also be a curse, as with S., who, struggle though he did, simply could not learn how to forget.

Like the imaginary Funes, he thought in images. Like Funes, he could not get past the visual details that flooded his brain, in order to grasp the meaning behind the details. This was a man who *really* could not see the forest for the trees.

When he tried to read, every word summoned up a separate, graphic image, creating chaos. He could not generalize, he could not categorize, he could not interpret experience. He could only remember it in literal, photographic terms.

In fact, this is how memory operates in babies, in this literal way. "The concept is that when you're an infant," Dr. Relkin says, "you can retain a literal representation of your sensory experiences, but you have no ability to put it together in any kind of meaningful sequence, out of the order in which it actually occurred."

In young childhood, he explains, you start being able to put things together, but "You have to be seven or eight before you really have the ability to tell a story out of temporal sequence. And then you go a little further and begin to speak symbolically, and to extract themes from your story, rather than necessarily remembering literally what happened. So that the direction of development is toward being able to encode bigger and bigger representations but less and less detail. It's the price that you pay: To be able to formulate abstractions and think symbolically, you have to give up that primary, eidetic kind of memory."

S. paid precisely the opposite price: He kept his incredible memory but gave up — not that he had any choice — normal development. What his extraordinary memory had created, Dr. Luria tells us, was a mind that was a junk heap.

Many years ago, in *The New York Times Magazine,* I wrote a profile of the man who was then the city's chief coroner, the legendary Milton Helpern. I described how he showed me a slide of a murder victim's face, close-up view, an eyeball delicately suspended upon the cheekbone. "It looks like one of those surreal paintings by Dalí," Dr. Helpern said. "Here's life imitating art."

Life imitating art. The memory came flooding back when I read about Funes, with his "garbage-heap" mind, a total fiction written almost a quarter century before the true case history of S., with his "junk-heap" mind. Here's art anticipating life.

Sometimes, lying in bed at night, reviewing what I recall of the day's events and trying, unsuccessfully, to remember what I had for lunch, I am able for a sweet fleeting moment to become positively Holmesian in my outlook.

Listen, I think, *forget* it. Unaccustomed as I am to blessing my own forgetfulness, let me be thankful not to remember what I had for lunch. There is no earthly reason to remember it. Holmes didn't need to recite the menu for purposes of his work or his life, and I don't need it for mine.

Let me be glad that, having met you once, I promptly forgot the color of your eyes, information that is equally inessential to my well-being. Let me rejoice that I do not recall every face I pass in the street, every word on a dictionary page, every name in a crowded room. True, I often screw up, as Holmes never does. I remember what I don't need to remember and forget what I don't want to forget, which I suppose makes my own mind a bit of a junk heap. I should work on that. But while I do so, let me remember to be glad that I *can* forget.

A blessing, all things considered.

CHAPTER FOUR:
HE REMEMBERS, SHE REMEMBERS
GENDER AND MEMORY

Poring over a crossword puzzle on a recent lazy Sunday morning, I ask my husband, "Would you happen to remember the name of a famous receiver for the Forty Niners, in nine letters?"

"Of *course*," he says, though he is not always such a fast draw on names. "Jerry Rice."

Of *course*, the man says. But I do not happen to remember who was a famous receiver for the Forty Niners. What I happen to remember is the gown that I wore to my senior prom. It was black tulle. It had a fuchsia satin midriff and an off-the-shoulder neckline, and the sleeves were . . .

But enough. The point I want to make, as I go tiptoeing through this minefield, is that there are plenty of women who are crazy for football and totally indifferent to clothes, but we are talking *averages* here (as in, *on* *average,* women are shorter than men),* and those women are not average. I am average. The sleeves were short and puffy, with little black bows.

This is the sort of thing that used to be called, on a broad base of no scientific evidence whatever, proof of "women's nature" and "men's nature." The nature theory has not been popular in recent decades — certainly not since the rebirth of the feminist movement, for which the idea of innate sex differences, except for your basic anatomical ones, is deeply politically incorrect. But science trumps politics, and brain-scan technology — PET (positron-emission tomography) and fMRI (functional magnetic resonance imaging) — which lets researchers actually *see* our minds at work, has given new steam to the old nature-nurture debate.

Slews of psychological tests in recent years show specific gender differences in memory. What they do not show is the cause. Among the differences:

* A little *averages* nugget to tuck away for those moments when the conversation lags (or when you forget what you were going to say): At the height of five foot ten, there are thirty men to every woman; at six feet, there are two thousand.

Men have better spatial memory and navigational ability, while women have better visual memory. Which means that, when negotiating how to get from here to there, men rely more on directional cues; women rely more on landmarks.

Women generally do better in what psychologists call *episodic memory,* as in "When was the last time we saw the Joneses?" And this is an edge that we seem to hold even into very old age, by which time the question may well be, "When was the last time we saw the Whatsisnames?"

Women have better eyewitness memory, as, for instance, in reporting the details of a violent accident or crime. Most of the great private eyes of literature may be male, but in real life women are, on average, more Sherlock Holmesian than men.

Women have better memory for autobiographical events. Among children, too, girls remember autobiographical events better than boys.

Women have better memory for experiences related to people. One study suggests that, even at an age of just a few months, most baby girls can remember people they know and are able to distinguish their photographs from the photographs of strangers. Baby boys generally cannot.

Females have better memory for emotion-related experiences, both positive and negative. We recall all these in much greater detail than men do. Some findings even indicate that we are better at remembering names, although you could never prove it by me.

Here is where the nature-nurture debate arises: Why should these gender differences exist?

It could, of course, be totally due to learned stereotypical behavior. If males show weaker verbal memory and weaker emotional memory, it could be because males are encouraged to say less and button up more. If they are better at remembering how to navigate a route, it may be because that is what men in our culture are supposed to do, just as females are supposed to be better at remembering interpersonal experiences.

Or it may be that our cultural conditioning actually affects the way our brains work, that a brain learns to remember more efficiently the things it is expected to remember.

Or it may be a mixed bag of cultural and biological factors.

My own bias has always been with the nurture school: Sex differences are due mainly to the social engineering that begins on day one in the hospital maternity ward, when they assign those pink and blue ID bracelets. If my husband remembers his first car (as he does, in loving detail) and I remember my first kiss (as I do, in CinemaScope), it is because those are the things that males and females in our society are expected to remember.

That is what I have always believed, and I had never seen evidence to the contrary. So I was riveted by an article that appeared on the op-ed page of *The New York Times* a couple of years ago, making the case for nature. It was written by an eminent psychiatrist and psychologist, Dr. Simon Baron-Cohen, who is the director of the Autism Research Centre at the University of Cambridge in England.

At that time, a war was raging in another Cambridge, in Massachusetts. In case you had been drifting on an ice floe in Antarctica and therefore happened not to hear about it, the facts were these:

The then-president of Harvard, Lawrence H. Summers, had suggested in a speech that women might be innately less suited than men to excel in math and science. Yikes! Lava flowed in Harvard Yard. Many of the faculty, and beyond, wanted Summers drawn and quartered, tarred and feathered, or at least fired. He held on for six months through the gathering storm, then resigned. (The outrage lingered on, and it is believed by some that this was not *necessarily* unrelated to the fact that in 2007 Drew Gilpin Faust was appointed the first woman president of Harvard in its 371-year history. "Harvard's waited a long time — since 1636," said one euphoric female professor.)

Dr. Baron-Cohen began his essay by asking, Had the president of Harvard gotten a bad rap? And proceeded to give the definitive answer: yes and no.

Yes, he said, testing for sex differences may show male superiority in the sciences. But testing reflects only averages. Testing cannot tell us anything about individuals — "which means that if you are a woman, there is no evidence to suggest that you could not become a Nobel laureate in your chosen area of scientific inquiry. A good scientist is a good scientist regardless of sex."

Having set out this nice caveat, as ex-President Summers might wish that he himself had done, Dr. Baron-Cohen moved on to the big *However:*

However, many psychological tests do show that, *on average* (a holy phrase in this research area), males do better in math, mechanics, physics — in understanding systems. (He defines a system as being any process governed by if-then rules: *If* you do *X* to *Y, then* you will get *Z.* Music, sailing, engineering, computer programming — they are all systems.) Females on average do better in language, communications, social relations, emotional perception — in understanding people.

Does conditioning play a role in all this? Absolutely, he says, but some differences are seen so early in life that biology must play a role, too. He goes back to *before* birth, to a process that starts *in utero,* with the flow of the hormone testosterone.

Testosterone is produced by both sexes, but far more by the male, and is involved in brain development. It is this hormone, Dr. Baron-Cohen believes, that determines whether we end up with a stronger drive toward understanding systems or understanding people. The higher the level of testosterone in the fetus, the likelier that the infant will develop what he calls a *system-izing* type brain. Extremely high levels may produce an "extreme male brain," characterized by the kind of obsessive interest in some systematic activity that is often associated with autism.

Systemizing. I fixed on that word.

I thought of the Argentinean writer Borges's fictional creation, Funes, a sort of *idiot savant* trapped in his own perfect memory.

I thought of S., the Russian psychologist Luria's patient, with his astounding memory.

I thought of those memory magicians performing onstage. Perhaps there have been the occasional women, but almost always they have been men, and all have used elaborate systems for memorizing.

I thought: Isn't memory facilitated by systemizing? Isn't mnemonics (from the Greek *mimneskesthai:* "to remember") based on systems? Mnemonics, in fact, *is* systems! Could this mean that men might be hardwired for different kinds of memory than women?

With this thought, I packed my questions into my luggage and went off to interview Dr. Baron-Cohen.

We met in his office, in one of those venerable Cambridge University buildings where the stairs creak and wood rails gleam with the patina of centuries.

Dr. Baron-Cohen is soft-spoken and gentle mannered, and he approaches the subject of gender differences with care.

Most researchers do, it being so fraught, but sometimes it gets frisky.

For example, in a debate at Harvard between psychologists Steven Pinker (nature) and Elizabeth Spelke (nurture), Dr. Pinker said, "It is said that there is a technical term for people who believe that little boys and little girls are born indistinguishable and are molded into their natures by parental socialization. The term is: *childless*." Pow!

(Few researchers, though, would be willing to go as audaciously — some would say outrageously — far out on the nature limb as Dr. Anne Moir, who co-authored a book with David Jessel, *Brain Sex: The Real Difference Between Men and Women,* in which she writes: "The sexes are different because their brains are different. The brain . . . is differently constructed in men and women; it processes information in a different way, which results in different perceptions, priorities and behavior." Findings that would support this view have been "quietly shelved," she says, because they are so politically incorrect. "But it is usually better to act on the basis of what is true, rather than to maintain, with the best will in the world, that what is true has no right to be so." No PC nonsense for Dr. Moir!)

I asked Dr. Baron-Cohen about the sex differences he has found at such young ages that they appear to be biological. He said, "It's hard to rule out environment unless you can either test at birth or relate it to prenatal factors, but we do see differences extremely early in development."

He mentioned a test in which his research team videotaped one-year-olds playing on the floor. Given a choice of films to watch, one of a face, one of cars (here we go again with cars), the boy babies looked longer at the cars; the girls, at the face.

Well, one-year-olds. I was not impressed. Plenty of conditioning can be done in that first year of life.

But in the next test that Dr. Baron-Cohen described, more than a hundred babies were videotaped while they were being shown two sights: a person's face, and a mechanical mobile of the same size, shape, and coloring as the face. The girls looked more at the face, the boys at the mobile.

"And this test was also done at age one year?" I said.

"No," he said, for I had misheard him. "At age one *day.*"

His researchers have tested infants whose prenatal testosterone levels could be measured in the frozen amniotic fluid of their mothers. At one year, those with the lower prenatal hormone levels, almost always the females, showed more eye contact, more communication skills, and generally more sociability. Those with the higher levels showed more interest in mechanical things.

In a follow-up study of these children at age four, the earlier findings held. The children who had the lower testosterone levels remained more advanced in language and social skills. Those who had the higher levels were less advanced socially and more restricted in their interests.

"When we got these results," Dr. Baron-Cohen writes in his book, *The Essential Difference: Male and Female Brains and the Truth About Autism,* "I had one of these strange feelings, like a shiver down the spine. A few drops more of this little chemical could affect your sociability or your language ability. I found it extraordinary."

My question, then: Could this "little chemical" also produce gender differences in memory?

It was not a question that Dr. Baron-Cohen had explored, nor does anyone else seem to have explored it in depth. But certainly the differences that show up in testing are the *kinds* of differences that fit his testosterone theory of the male-type brain, more attracted to things, and the female-type brain, more attracted to people.

I asked him: Do people who have the "extreme male brain," the type he associates with autism, tend to have better than average memories?

"Yes. Obviously, there are different kinds of memory. Studies suggest that people with autism may have a better memory for facts. They may not have a better memory for experiences.

"We did a study of teenagers who are talented mathematicians, winners of a competition called the United Kingdom Math Olympiad, and we had the opportunity to look at autistic traits in that group. They scored higher than average."

"How did they break down by gender?" I asked.

"Mostly male."

"Slightly? Predominantly?"

"Overwhelmingly."

To say that autistic people have a better memory for facts is not at all the same as saying that *males* have a better memory for facts; but autistic males outnumber autistic females ten to one.

Why should any of this be so?

Suppose, for the moment, that nature plays a role, perhaps courtesy of that "little chemical." Suppose that sex differences are at least partly inborn, that the average male is just plain naturally better in the realm of things, and the average female is better in the realm of people. If you put your money on Darwin, as I put mine, you have to wonder: In evolutionary terms, in which survival of the species is the ultimate name of the game, what purpose might such differences serve?

Evolutionary theories are notoriously difficult to prove or disprove, but often they seem reasonable beyond reasonable doubt. Imagine, for example, those ancestors of ours venturing out to do the hunting and tracking. It certainly would have been vital for them to understand the mechanics of things.

"When you're talking about Stone Age times," Dr. Baron-Cohen says, "about how to make a flint, for example, if one could very quickly notice how small differences in the angle of that flint might make it a more efficient tool, that could have some evolutionary benefit."

Just as it would have been vital for those who were back at home base, tending the children and dependent upon the community for support, to be well attuned to people.

"In evolutionary terms, the two sexes lived in very different worlds. Where we are today may reflect the evolutionary pressures on the sexes way back then."

Consider that super-well-documented sex difference in memory: better spatial memory for men, better visual memory for women.

In evolutionary terms, it makes total sense. When that Stone Age man went forth to bring home the bacon, a good memory for direction would have come in a lot handier than a good memory for landmarks. When I think of a landmark, I think of the gas station opposite the supermarket, the first stop sign after the traffic light, the movie theater down at the east end of the mall. Not many unmistakable landmarks in the vast, undifferentiated stretches of the prehistoric plain or jungle.

But today! What grabs me about this particular sex difference is its application today. *Finally,* here is the answer to what I have always considered to be one of the great mysteries of life: Why do so many marital spats take place in cars?

You know the script. It is etched into the upholstery of our family car and the cars of my innumerable interviewees, and seems always to go like this:

HE: I *know* we're going in the right direction. We're heading due north.

SHE: I *know* we should turn around. We passed that church ten minutes ago.

Typically followed by escalation, followed by silence, followed by arrival at destination extremely late.

At last (at least), I understand. The fault is not in us but (possibly) in our testosterone, or lack thereof.

It is good to understand this. It is also good to keep in mind that one way of remembering how to get from here to there is not *necessarily* better than the other. They are simply different ways of viewing the landscape — both the outer one and the inner.

P.S. I consider it my duty and pleasure to report that, on the very day of my interview with Dr. Baron-Cohen, just after we had finished, this happened: I boarded a train going from Cambridge back to London, began reading a London newspaper, and what did I come upon? Oh, yes. A major news story about a national math-puzzle contest, the *Times* National Su Doku Championship. I quote:

"Nina Pell, 18, a university student from

Wales, made easy work of a super-fiendish puzzle, leaving the men trailing in her wake. Even by the time the 255 entrants had been whittled down to six for the grand final, women outnumbered men by two to one, and they took first, second and fourth places, demolishing the common belief that men are better than women at maths."

So much for averages.

P.P.S. No typographical error: "Maths" is how the Brits say it.

CHAPTER FIVE:
I'M DANCING AS
FAST AS I CAN
EXERCISE AND MEMORY

I live with a man who goes to bed cheery and wakes up testy. He makes his breakfast, he washes the dishes, he gets lost in the newspaper. It cannot be said that he encourages conversation.

An hour after breakfast, he goes to the gym. He stays there forty minutes, and when he comes back, *mirabile dictu,* he is cheery again.

It's the exercise, he says. The exercise wakes up his brain.

Wakes up his brain. Can he elaborate?

He can: "When I get up in the morning, I'm in a daze. I can't think clearly. I'm logy; I'm dim-witted; all I can do is sit quietly and read. My body is awake, but my brain is still asleep. And then, *then,* I go down to the gym and I do my twenty minutes on the treadmill, and I do my weights, and suddenly everything's clear! I can think! My brain wakes up!"

He says that he hears this from other regular exercisers: Their brains wake up. *Regular* — that is the operative word. This man is in the gym every other day. Not rain, nor snow, nor a lazy Sunday morning, nor a rotten head cold, nor whatever it was that could not sway the postman from his appointed rounds — nothing can keep my husband from his alternate-day exertions in the gym.

Me? I make resolutions, which is something I am very good at. I have New Year's resolutions for every day of the year. In this particular matter, I resolve to exercise tomorrow. It could hardly be more convenient, since we live in an apartment building that has a well-equipped gym in the basement. But when tomorrow comes, there are usually compelling reasons to do other things, so I will exercise instead the day after tomorrow. Unless other compelling reasons arise, as they usually do.

Or so it had always been, until the discovery of certain facts about exercise and memory that were news to me, and may be to you as well.

Come back for a bit to that holy quartet of imperatives that the memory experts keep touting: a healthy diet, a good night's rest, avoidance of stress, and regular exercise, both physical and mental.

As for diet and rest, is there anyone out there who does not know about the efficacy of high protein and low fat and sound sleep? We needn't belabor it.

As to the stress factor, good luck. I wish I could help you with that one, but I have trouble enough with my own stress factor, never mind anyone else's.

But as to exercise, research — the kind of research that was impossible to do until *very* recent years — has handed us some surprises.

The first surprise: Mental exercise does not *necessarily* cut the mustard.

Just as physical exercise nourishes the body, mental exercise nourishes the mind. Nobody disputes that. But an authoritative long-range study called ACTIVE, in which almost three thousand older adults had training to sharpen their memory, reasoning ability, and speed of processing new information, turned up a mixed bag of results.

The researchers found that memory training did indeed improve memory, but it could not slow the rate of normal memory loss. Further, the improvement was selective. People who were trained in such tasks as remembering lists of words and remembering the main points of stories did show better memory — for doing those kinds of tasks. But the improvement did not seem to carry over into the conduct of everyday life. In other words, you can do those crossword puzzles until you're seeing grids in your sleep, and discover many dandy new words (and possibly even remember them), but the exercise may not do much to help you remember where you parked the car.

Which will not keep me from doing crossword puzzles. First, because I like crossword puzzles. And second because, next year, the researchers may say something else. They do that a lot in the health sciences. Think of the flip-flops on annual mammography, hormone-replacement therapy, anti-inflammatory drugs. Next year, they may find out that mental exercise does nothing much for memory but has some other happy application. (As happened with the drug L-dopa, that was developed to treat Parkinson's disease but had the altogether unforeseen effect of making some victims horny. Whether this was considered a happy application, I do not know and would just as soon not ask.)

Or they may simply find out that they were wrong — that mental exercise is the very best thing you can do for your memory.

In fact, Yaakov Stern, the neuropsychologist at Columbia University Medical Center, believes that this one is still a wide-open question. While other researchers have tested whether exercising the mind can improve memory in older adults, Professor Stern is designing programs for younger people, to test whether cognitive exercise can stave off, or even prevent, age-related memory loss. The market is overrun now with cognitive-exercise programs that make great claims but produce few lasting results, as I discuss in Chapter Seventeen. But Dr. Stern thinks it may be that researchers simply haven't yet come up with the right kinds of cognitive exercise.

The second surprise: Physical exercise does not *necessarily* cut the mustard, either — except when it does. And when it does, it works splendidly. It all depends on what kind of exercise you do.

We have always understood in a vague, intuitive way that physical exercise is "good" for us, whatever that means. As recently as the nineties, it was assumed to mean that it is beneficial in a general way to general health.

Beyond that, exercisers have learned by the doing what the scientists have learned from the testing: that "good" also means the shot in the arm that regular exercise seems to give to the brain. How does it happen? Why does it happen? Exercisers don't know. They only know that it happens.

In fact, even researchers did not know much more until the development of brain-scanning technology that makes it possible to see not only the structure of the brain but also precisely which parts of that structure are activated by different kinds of stimulation.

Today, brain scanning has been absorbed into the vast medical armamentarium without much fuss or awareness among us lay folk. Medical people no longer seem to make much fuss, either; after all, they are waist deep in technology. But it is this extraordinary technology that has opened up the whole amazing, revelatory field of human neuroscience — a field that truly exploded in the nineties.

Neuroscience itself is about a hundred years old. But until brain scanning came along, it was mostly restricted to experimental animal research, for the obvious reason that you could not see what was going on inside the living, functioning human brain — not and stay within the law. The advent of brain-scanning technology has been — still is, with momentous discoveries popping up all the time, and with more momentous ones doubtless yet to come — a true revolution. I will put my money on future generations' looking back upon this technology as the greatest advancement in knowledge of human behavior since Freud developed his theory of the unconscious. Alas, I won't be around to collect.

So here is what brain-scan studies have taught us that we couldn't have known before about the effects of different kinds of physical exercise upon cognition:

Stretching and toning are good. No one can say they're not good. I sit for hours each day with my nose pressed to the computer screen, and soon my poor arthritic back is yowling in protest. If I get up and do just five minutes' worth of stretching exercises, it works wonders for my back. But it does nothing for my brain. You can stretch and tone all day and doubtless it will do all sorts of desirable things for you, your muscles, your bones, your flexibility and balance, your general physical well-being, and probably, at least temporarily, your level of stress. But there is no evidence that it does anything impressive for your cognition.

Aerobics does.

When I first heard this, I was mystified in the same way as I have always been mystified by, say, aspirin: How does aspirin *know* to go to that part of the body that is hurting? And just so with aerobics: How could one particular kind of physical exercise — but not another! — have an effect on my brain? How did my brain *know* to respond to that kind of exercise and *only* that kind?

I put the obvious question to Dr. Stern: "It must happen because aerobics sends more oxygen to the brain, right?"

From a journalist's perspective, Stern is a jewel. He is user-friendly, by which I mean that he can do what scientists and academics often cannot — translate the abstruse language of their callings into human-speak for the benefit of the rest of us.

"More oxygen, yes, that's one idea," he said. "But the big thing, the main thing, is chemical. There have been controlled studies of normal older people, where they gave them aerobic exercises and stretching and toning exercises, and the aerobics had disproportionate benefits in brain function. There's this chemical compound called BDNF" (Brain-derived neurotrophic factor, if you must know) "which seems to help various processes that are involved in learning something new. And what they have found is, aerobic exercise generates more of this chemical!"

And then I do my twenty minutes on the

treadmill, and I do my weights, and suddenly everything's clear! I can think! My brain wakes up!

"It's chemistry that makes the neurons work well," Stern said. "How the neurons talk to one another, how they develop new connections . . . that's all chemicals and proteins." And here he explained how those neurons *do* talk to one another in such a way that even I was able to understand it:

"The neuron is a specialized brain cell that has two parts. One part receives information. The other part sends the information to another neuron. So it's like a fancy wiring process. Very complex wiring. The transmission of information from one part of the neuron to the other — that's electric. But the transmission *between* neurons, the way one neuron speaks to another, is chemical. The neuron releases a chemical, a neurotransmitter, into a synapse — that's the gap between neurons — and that chemical stimulates the next neuron. And when that neuron is stimulated to the right degree, it creates a little electric charge, and the charge travels. You can imagine many, many neurons converging on one, and really stirring a neurotransmitter, and at some point that will cause this neuron to fire."

Hmm. "Sort of like an orgasm," I said.

The professor considered my little scientific contribution. He laughed. "Yeah, it's like that," he said. "A cognition orgasm."

There are *a hundred billion* neurons doing their stuff in there, firing away. I don't know how anyone counts them. I *do* know that this is considered a conservative estimate — some researchers think there may be as many as two hundred billion or more. And there are *trillions* (some say *hundreds* of trillions, but when you get into that stratosphere, what difference?) of synapses. And they are in constant play, networks of neurons and synapses forming and fading, forming and fading, and the stronger those networks, the more robust this ceaseless electrical and chemical activity, the more robust the brain.

We get older and the forming continues, but the fading may begin to outpace it. So you can see that anything that ramps up the action is going to be good for our memories.

The third surprise: Aerobic exercise does not simply improve "memory" — nothing that imprecise. It sets out like a homing pigeon, like my mystery aspirin, to improve *exactly* those kinds of memory that begin giving us trouble in middle age, such as our old nemesis multitasking.

Now, multitasking is a function of the

frontal lobes of the brain. As I've said, these are among the first areas of the brain to be affected by aging, which is why multitasking becomes difficult. Also, as I've said, brain cells die and new ones are generated through our lifetimes but the generation slows down as we age — and in some parts of the brain, as in the frontal lobes, it seems to slow down to a halt.

"There used to be a big controversy about the generation of new cells," Dr. Stern said. "Did it happen in just one part of the brain, or in other parts as well? Now it appears that it happens only in the hippocampus, which is so important to memory."

Some research suggests that it happens also in the olfactory bulb, where we identify odors.

"Well, then," I said, "if new cells are not being generated in the frontal lobes, how can the multitasking function be improved by aerobic exercise?"

"Because of this chemical BDNF that is generated by aerobics. It supports the survival of the cells that are already there."

Researchers used to believe that what caused our memory problems were the changes in particular brain areas — the loss of neurons that occurs with normal aging. But the emphasis has shifted. Now they put greater stress on the changes in communication *between* brain areas. It is not just the number of neurons that matter but the number and strength of connections between them. (In fact, the loss of neurons is no longer considered so significant. We may lose many millions each day; big deal, given what's in there.) It is these synaptic connections that start losing numbers and potency with normal aging, and the theory is that aerobics gives them, so to speak, that chemical shot in the arm.

The effect of aerobics on mental performance has been shown in many experiments with animals (primarily rats, which you might not even want to know, but give it a chance. To learn that when wheels are put into rats' cages and they are allowed to run their little hearts out upon these wheels, they then perform certain cognitive tasks faster and better than rats who are just lying around doing nothing — to learn this is not uninteresting and not without a moral for us humanoids). But the breakthrough work with people like us has been done by Arthur F. Kramer, professor of neuroscience and psychology at the University of Illinois at Urbana-Champaign, and his colleagues.

Dr. Kramer's team has taken groups of

volunteers ranging from middle age to elderly, all in good health, all leading moderately sedentary lives, and put them into six-month exercise-training programs. Some participants did aerobic exercise — essentially, walking — and some did toning exercises.

"Any surprises?" I asked Kramer.

"Yes, the results," he said, putting not too wordy a point on it. "We found that if you were in the walking group, you could perform certain cognitive tasks fifteen to twenty percent faster than if you were in the toning group. That finding really surprised us."

Fifteen to twenty percent! They were surprised? I was *stunned.* I asked, "Did people have to walk fast to get that result?"

"No. Just walk. They started out slowly, walking fifteen minutes a day, and worked up to an hour three times a week."

The Kramer studies were the first to measure improvement in doing specific tasks that are called, in the trade, *executive control processes.* Such tasks are all functions of that frontal lobe area of the brain where aging occurs first. In addition to multitasking, they include planning, scheduling, paying attention, and blocking out distractions. (According to some research, the distractions are a bigger problem than the lack of attention.)

Executive control processes also include something called stopping, or, in the jargon, aborting preplanned responses. I asked for an cxample, and Kramer said, "If you're driving, and you're ready to make a left-hand turn, and you suddenly see a pedestrian in your path . . ."

Understood.

Before the exercise-training program began, the subjects had all been tested for their performance in these tasks. When it ended, and they were tested again, the walkers turned out to be way ahead of the toners — walking proof that when our biology slows down on the job, we can do much of the job for ourselves.

Think of it: fifteen to twenty percent improvement in multitasking, planning, scheduling, paying attention to the matter at hand, blocking out distractions, and aborting that perilous left-hand turn.

Oh, and one thing more: "We found, in an analysis of the scientific literature," Kramer said, "that *the combination of both aerobics and weight-lifting had even greater cognitive benefits.*" (Italics mine.)

Well, you can imagine. Since I got the word, I'm out there three times a week, hitting the treadmill, hoisting weights, and dancing (although, as Kramer said, you don't *need* to go fast) as fast as I can.

Which is not to shortchange mental exercise. Because whatever it may or may not do for memory, it just feels so good when it works.

On the edge of sleep one recent night, I suddenly thought of three friends I had to contact in the morning: Ina, Molly, and Toby. I reached to switch on the light and make a note. Then I thought, *No, damn it, remember. Okay, but how? Most obvious, play with the initials. I-M-T? Nothing. T-I-M? Nah — just another name to forget. M-I — hold it, now. Hold it. M-I-T! My brother went to MIT! That's my association!* (And association, remember, is the name of the game.)

And the next morning, there it was: M-I-T. Made my three calls. Made me feel stronger, surer, keener. Made me feel *good* as I pumped my eight pounders and ran (well, fast-walked) my twenty-minute mile.

CHAPTER SIX:
A MEDITATION ON
THE ELEPHANT
THE THINGS WE NEVER FORGET

Ask a dozen people — as I have asked many dozens — "What are the personal experiences that you will never forget?" and they will tell you pretty much what you would expect to hear: my mother's death, my daughter's birth, the day I was married, the day I was divorced, the day the house burned down, the day I learned that that bastard (alternatively, bitch) was cheating on me . . . The usual.

But stick with it, peel away a few more onion-skin layers of recollection, and eventually you will hit pay dirt. Pay dirt will be a memory from childhood that even today — thirty, forty, sixty years after the event — still sears the soul. And what may amaze you about this unforgettable memory is that, *to you,* it sounds so eminently forgettable, so mundane, even trivial, that you cannot imagine why it has stuck to the psyche in such a tenacious way. But then, we have trouble enough understanding our own psyches, never mind anyone else's.

Why should some memories cling so stubbornly?

Yes, yes, we understand: The more emotional the experience has been, the more persistent the memory will be. We understand that much intuitively. But *why?* On the biological level, what is going on?

On that level, it is pure chemistry.

Tucked cozily into the curve of the hippocampus is that little almond-shaped powerhouse, the amygdala, mediator of emotions, "the emotional computer of the brain," the Harvard psychologist Daniel L. Schacter calls it. The amygdala signals fear, say, and the stress-related hormones go into action. The pulse quickens, the limbs feel trembly, the body temperature changes, the chest feels heavy with a kind of premonitory unease, and there is that sudden rush of *something* into the throat.

It is the adrenaline flowing. The greater the fear, the more the adrenaline flows, and the more the adrenaline flows, the deeper that memory will be embedded. Can't pry it out of there with a crowbar.

Deeply, deeply etched into that tangle of tissue and wires where long-term memory lives, are the traumas of childhood. The joys, too. But it is any kind of injury to the senses — an insult; a rejection; a rivalry; an embarrassment, even a minor one — that seems to have the strongest staying power.

Try sibling resentment.

A noted psychoanalyst told me once of a patient who complained that his parents had favored his elder brother. He was forever whining and whimpering about this brother, and one day, as proof, he brought in a snapshot of himself and his sibling taken at ages four and six, both holding Easter baskets. "There, you see!" he said triumphantly. "Just look at how much bigger his basket is than mine!"

The patient was thirty-five.

Here is a sixty-one-year-old man, talking about his twin brother:

We were seven or eight. We were roughhousing, and he banged into one of those things that hold knick-knacks and broke a glass vase. He went yelling to my mother, "Danny broke your vase!" I said, "I did not! *He* did it." But she didn't believe me because the week before, I *had* broken something and she had given me a big lecture about carelessness. And when my father came home she said, "Danny broke a vase," and I got whacked. I wanted to kill my brother. I wanted to kill my father and mother, too. I can still taste that terrible taste of *injustice.* For a long time, I had these major murderous fantasies.

Try helplessness. A friend — these are mostly uncomfortable stories and their owners wanted not to be named — remembers:

I was five years old. I was out in front of the house playing dress-up with my mother's pocketbook and gloves. Two bigger kids took the pocketbook from me and started to toss it to each other over my head, like a ball. And I'm running back and forth, back and forth, trying to grab it, and they're laughing and going "nyah nyah," and I began to cry.

Recalling this, five decades later, she gets teary. "Oh, God, the rage I felt. *Impotent rage.* All my life, that is the feeling I just can't handle, the feeling that drives me totally crazy — impotent rage. And I've always been convinced that it must be because of that day."

Try embarrassment:

I was eight. I saw three grown women — fifteen or sixteen, I guess — on the other side of the street, jitter-bugging. I tried to imitate them. I did a few tiny steps. Then I looked up and saw that they had stopped dancing and they were pointing at me and doubled up laughing. I ran home. I thought I would die of humiliation. I can still hear them laughing, the little bitches.

This woman is sixty-eight. Having told me the story, she then sent me an e-mail describing the little bitches seen sixty years ago.

Try wounded pride:

It was the one time I was ever spanked. I was five years old and we were eating supper and I was in a pissy mood for some reason. I deliberately spilled sugar on the floor. My father mopped it up and said that if I did it again, he would spank me. So I did it again, and he put me over his knee and spanked me, not hard but *in front of my brothers!*

I said, "I'm leaving!" and I ran to my room and got my favorite sweater, which was purple, and my favorite doll, and I wrapped them in a sort of knapsack and I ran out and got as far as the corner. Then I stopped to review my options. It was October, and it was getting dark. I remember thinking, "It'll be completely dark soon, and I'm hungry." So I went back.

Years later, my mother told me they'd kept watching me out the window all the time. They told all their friends. Very funny.

Louise, age fifty-three, still fails to see what's so funny.

Now here is a sad little leaf from my own book, and please hold the laughter:

I am in second grade. Miss Palm, whom we adore, has brought in a bowl of autumn leaves in high color. Each of us has the pleasure, the inestimable delight, of choosing her very own leaf. We will then paste them to sheets of paper.

Miss Palm squeezes some paste onto each sheet. Soon I am out of paste. I raise my hand for more. Again I run short, and again raise my hand.

"Martha!" she says. "What's the problem? Everyone else has enough paste."

Oh, shame. Now I see the problem: The others are putting dabs of paste on their leaves, a dab here, a dab there, while I am trying to cover its entire surface. Girls are giggling.

"Tell me," repeats Miss Palm, "what is the problem?"

Tell her? I cannot speak. I cannot breathe. I want to die, and surely will, of stupidity.

End of story. What's yours?

Physical pain clings to memory, too, but in a different way. My brother can recall the pain that he felt when some neighborhood bully beat him up, nearly breaking his arm, more than a half century ago. But much more vivid is his memory of the sense of shame that this happened to him in front of other kids and that our mother came out to protect him.

Physical pain is merely remembered; emotional pain can be fully reexperienced — a curious distinction that I will explore in Chapter Nine.

"The date is June 17, 1959. I am twelve years old. The Novocain didn't work like it should, so they hold me down in the chair and they pull two teeth."

My friend does not simply tell it like this, she transports herself back to the moment and takes me there with her. "They were supposed to pull four, my twelve-year molars, but they only got two because I passed out."

I am horrified. "Your mother didn't stop them?"

"She wasn't there. The nanny had dropped me off. I was there alone."

"But afterward? When you told her?"

"I never told her. I never told anyone. I couldn't talk about it for thirty years, it was so emotionally devastating."

Memories needn't be painful to stick to the ribs. The Cornell University neurologist Norman Relkin says, "Patients sometimes ask, 'How come I can't remember what I had for lunch, but I remember what I had at my tenth-birthday party?' Well, some memory tasks are inherently more difficult than others. And people who are uncertain whether they're getting a memory disorder often don't distinguish among these things. They will fail in a recollection and be worried by it. But part of the challenge is recognizing that not all types of recollection are equally easy. Events that occur repeatedly, in stereotyped fashion, like lunches, are very hard to remember. The first thing the brain does is put them into the category of lunches, and you have thousands of those, if not tens of thousands."

But there is just one tenth-birthday party.

The unconscious is an overstuffed closet. We do not ever come anywhere close to a full awareness of what is in there, labeled

The Things I Will Never Forget.

Why should I wake up from a dream, saying aloud, "324–3074" — my mother's telephone number, which I haven't dialed (remember *dialing?*) in more than two decades?

If someone had asked me, "What was your mother's telephone number?" I would have said, "Why on earth should I remember such a thing? My mother has been dead for twenty-four years." But there it was, alive and pulsing, in my unconscious.

Why should my husband come into the kitchen one morning, still bleary-eyed, and announce, apropos of nothing whatever, "19204376"? His Army Air Corps serial number. From 1946.

I said, "What made you think of that?"

"I don't know."

"Were you dreaming?"

"I don't know."

"Would you have remembered it if I had asked?"

"No way."

Psychologists speak of *deep-storage memory*. When it gets that deep, you might call it deep-freeze. But it can surface and thaw on a dime.

These personal experiences that we so persistently remember are often experiences that we would be nothing but happy to forget. But here is the irony: This is exactly the type of memory that is largely unaffected by aging. You may be forgetting the paperboy's name, forgetting where you left your eyeglasses, forgetting what errands you have to run in the morning and who told you what last night, but time has done nothing to help you forget the mortification you felt when you wet your pants in first grade.

A friend says that her mother never got over precisely that experience. It had happened when she was six and it still haunted her in her seventies:

Her own mother, my grandmother, didn't believe in public education. She wanted to teach her kids at home, but the city officials made her send them to public school. On my mother's very first day, she raised her hand to go to the bathroom, and the teacher said, "We just had recess. You can't go now."

So she wet her pants, and my grandmother had to come and get her, and that was the end of her public school education. She talked about that to the very end of her life but not as a funny story. It was still painful.

"Your memory is informed by emotion," says Gayatri Devi, the New York neurologist and psychiatrist. "Emotion is as important for memory as . . . well, as memory itself! If fact and emotion were diagrammed, they would, in my opinion, contribute equally to what gets stored in your brain."

Ask professional actors, of whom I have interviewed a good many, what has caused the most humiliating memories of their lives, and the answer is often just this: *memory.* Failure of same.

Well, of course. How could it not be?

If you and I are talking and you forget what you were about to say, so what? Another thought will be along in a minute. But if you stand frozen on that stage beneath lights bright enough to catch every glint of fear in your eye, exposed to a black maw filled with hundreds of customers who have paid good money (and, on Broadway, obscene amounts of it) to see you perform — if you, in that circumstance, suddenly forget your lines . . . Oh, Lord. I don't even want to try to imagine what that must be like.

Going up, they call it. It is the terror that comes with the territory.

"It's like you *die.* I was in this show . . ." This is Priscilla Lopez, fifty-eight. If you were lucky enough to see the original production of *A Chorus Line,* back in the seventies, you saw Priscilla Lopez, and she has been working steadily ever since. "And I was doing my big song. And suddenly I forgot what came next. I thought, *'What's happened? Oh, my God'* — sweat dripping down my face — *'what comes next?'* It was like I was outside myself, looking at me standing there. It was terrible . . ."

As she says this, she replays the scene with brio, standing frozen, hands raised in panic to either side of a head in which the amygdala is going crazy and zillions of neurons are firing away like fireworks over Kansas City on a July Fourth night. Oh, it *is* terrible.

"And I just stopped dead. I just stood there and said, 'I can't. I can't. I can't.' And I walked offstage. One minute into a four-minute song, and I walked offstage. You just don't *do* that!

"Backstage was bedlam. Everyone scurrying around in panic, because it affects everything — music cues, light cues, actor cues, everything. It's a machine working in a certain order, and I jammed the works. Oh, God. That is my very worst memory."

"Women and elephants never forget an

injury." That's smart-mouthed talk from the writer Hector Hugo Munro (aka Saki).

And here is another, obviously on the same sentimental wavelength, from Lord Byron's *Don Juan:* "Sweet is revenge — especially to women."

I don't know how elephants got into the act (although it is true that they are thought to have keen memories), but forget the part about women.

Yes, there are sex differences in memory. But this is not one of them. Both sexes are plenty good at injury hoarding. If anything, the tilt is in the other direction: A recent study suggests that when it comes to nursing an insult, holding a grudge, or enjoying revenge, men have sharper memory than women.

The study was done in the Department of Imaging Neuroscience at University College London. The researchers paired up thirty-two subjects and had them play a game. If both partners played cooperatively, both won. But there were a few ringers in the group, actors who had been told to play selfishly. Soon everyone hated them. The subjects then were brain scanned while they watched various players getting zapped by mild electrical shock.

Whenever a cooperative player was

zapped, all the subjects showed sympathy — the empathy centers of their brains lit up.

Whenever a selfish player was zapped, all the men's brains registered pleasure. Vengeance!

The women? Their empathy centers kept glowing like glowworms.

People who work in the arts — actors, writers, artists, those whose work is reviewed by professional critics — have a remarkably good memory for bad reviews. I know many. Long after the fact, they can recall every unflattering adjective ever written about them. (Myself included? You bet.)

I was walking once in Manhattan's theater district with a friend, a theater critic, when a well-known character actor came striding toward us. My friend said a hearty hello. The actor strode right by, cutting him dead.

"What was that about?" I asked.

He said, "Twenty years ago I reviewed a play he was in, and I praised his performance except for one negative adjective. He's never forgiven me that adjective."

Recently I watched a tape of the actors Paul Newman and Robert Redford reminiscing on television about their early careers. It was shown not long before Newman announced his retirement, at age eighty-two. Neither his confidence nor his sense of invention nor his memory were any longer quite sharp enough, he said (sounding plenty sharp enough), to let him work at the level he demanded of himself. That saddened me, because Newman at less than the level he demands of himself is still a whole lot better than most.

But I was amused, and touched, to hear the golden boy Redford, for so long a critically celebrated star, recalling precisely what a major newspaper reviewer had written about one of his very first performances: "He said I was 'hammy and overwrought.' "

That had been many long decades before. Redford recalled it with a laugh but ruefully, lingering on the adjectives, the note of injured pride still floating there in the margins of his voice.

When you put this question, What personal experience will you never forget? to enough people, patterns emerge. I have found that for anyone who has ever been through it, there is one memory that tops the list of the unforgettable: bearing witness to the primal scene.

The detail! The vividness! Technicolor, wide-screen, Dolby sound. People who ever stumbled upon their parents making love tend to remember it decades later with photographic precision.

I am reporting this in full, as it was reported to me, because it comes from a seventy-eight-year-old woman who was eight when it happened, and in its very richness of detail is a pretty good example of the effect of emotion upon memory:

My parents took me to New York for the 1939 World's Fair. We stayed in a kind of crummy hotel with two tiny adjoining rooms, one with a double bed and one with a sofa bed. And I was scared to be alone in a strange place, so my mother slept on the sofa bed with me.

I woke up in the middle of the night and she wasn't there. I knew what was going on. I heard a loud squeaking noise and I knew it was that bed. I mean, I didn't know what they were *doing,* I didn't understand about sex yet — eight-year-old kids these days understand it, but I didn't — but I knew that I had been deserted and that she was in that bed with my father and I was mad at both of them.

So I marched into the other room. I could see everything. There was lots of light coming in from the street. A big neon sign right outside the window kept blinking. The bed kept squeaking away, and I saw this big white ass bouncing *up* and down, *up* and down, *up* and down, and it was like it was keeping time with the squeaking bed and the blinking light. I had absolutely no idea what it meant. But I was furious, and I said, in this loud, angry voice, "I *knew* you'd be here!"

Well, my mother's head came up off the pillow and she stared at me, and my poor daddy, his head just *whipped* around, and I will never forget that look of *sheer panic* on his face. He was frozen; he was just staring at me with that horrified expression. Then he sort of hopped off her and covered himself, and I marched back to the sofa bed and lay there in a real snit.

After a while my mother came in and began telling me how this was something married people did because they loved each other, and when I was older I would understand, and all that . . . but I wasn't having any of it. I just turned my face to the wall and wouldn't say a word. And we were there for two more days and I never said a word to my father and he never said a word to me. He couldn't even look at me, he was so embarrassed.

We never talked about it except once,

years and years later, when I was already married. And you know what? He still got beet red. He said, "Oh, you were so little. You don't really remember anything."

I said, "Oh, no? The bed was squeaking. A light was blinking outside. You had on just your pajama tops. They were blue-and-white striped."

Speak, memory.

CHAPTER SEVEN:
IT'S NOT KETCHUP
THE 57 VARIETIES OF MEMORY

JOE: We ate in a great restaurant last
  week.
CHARLIE: Yeah? What's the name of it?
JOE: I can't remember. It's sort of like . . .
  It sounds like . . . What's the name of
  that flower, the red one, with all the
  thorns?
CHARLIE: A rose?
JOE: That's it! A rose! Hey, Rose! (*yelling
  offstage*) What's the name of that restaurant we ate in last night?

Joe sounds like a bit of a lout and the joke
is terribly long in the tooth, but I still love
it. I love it for the way it takes two different
kinds of memory and rubs them together to
produce a laugh.

As Columbia University's neuropsychologist Yaakov Stern points out, psychologists
never speak simply of memory. They speak
of different kinds of memory, and these dif-

ferent kinds involve different parts of the brain — as we saw previously, with the effects of aerobic exercise upon the frontal lobes. But there is no tidy one-on-one. Memory is everywhere in the brain, and when you are storing or retrieving any particular kind of memory, many of the brain's parts get into the act.

It all gets enormously complex, and most of it, I'm happy to say, we have no need to know. It won't help us remember. Memory in its many varieties becomes, as the experts chart it, rather like a genealogical tree — with branches coming off the trunk and twigs coming off the branches and twiglets coming off the twigs and so forth — and what I want to do here is try to prune the damn thing, clear out the underbrush so that we can see the shape of it, grasp the basic idea, because when you can grasp the basic idea, you have more control. You don't work yourself into a sweat when you forget the name of the restaurant you ate in last week, because you know that it is a commonplace lapse and you know why. (If you forget the name of your spouse, that's a whole other story. I am not getting anywhere near that story.)

Let me say at the outset that not all types of memory are equally affected by aging.

Some are hardly affected at all. The one called episodic memory, soon to be described, is the most vulnerable to aging. And the one called *working memory,* also soon to be described, is limited for everyone, regardless of age.

Specialists argue about what belongs precisely where on this memory tree. But most of them agree that the tree has three main branches, or memory systems: *declarative* (or *explicit*) *memory,* working memory, and *nondeclarative* (or *implicit*) *memory.*

Declarative memory is memory that we consciously take in and consciously pull out. Or *try* to pull out, as in "It's on the tip of my tongue." Facts, faces, words, events, personal and impersonal experiences . . . most of what we know about the world and about ourselves belongs to the declarative-memory system.

Coming off this declarative branch of the tree are two major secondary branches: semantic memory and episodic memory.

Semantic memory covers, essentially, facts:

The Empire State Building is in New York City.
Friday follows Thursday.
A poodle is a breed of dog.

A restaurant is a place where you go to eat.

Episodic memory covers whatever is part of personal experience:

We took a tour of the Empire State Building.
Thank God it's Friday!
My dog is (alas, was, dear sweet girl) a black standard poodle named Gwendolyn.
We ate in a great restaurant last week.

Which brings us back to the Rose joke. When Joe cannot remember the name of the restaurant he visited last week, that is a lapse of episodic memory, and he needn't worry about it, just join the crowd. That is the boat we are all in.

When he cannot remember the name of his wife of thirty years, that is a lapse of semantic memory, and Joe should worry. So should Rose. Because most names, including the names of casual acquaintances, the names of people you just met, the names of people you infrequently see or think about — in short, the names of non-intimates — all those generally belong in episodic memory. But the name of a longtime spouse, like the names of your parents, your siblings, your children, people whose names you know as well as your own, should be carved in the concrete of semantic memory.

So either Joe has a real memory problem, or Joe and Rose have a real marital problem. Or both.

Semantic memory is tenacious. Even into very old age, it hangs in there. Whereas episodic memory is the mischievous wretch that starts playing no-show games with us typically around age fifty, give or take a few years and a few hundred million nerve cells. (No big loss, as I've pointed out — not when the brain is estimated to have from one to two hundred *billion* of them.)

For a simple illustration of the difference between these two kinds of declarative memory, try the difference between "What are eyeglasses?" and "Where did I leave my eyeglasses?"

That says it.

Semantic knowledge, like remembering the dishes that have been in your kitchen forever, is stored mainly in the back part of the brain. But knowledge that involves a particular context, like remembering what kind of food you ate off those dishes last Sunday, is managed primarily in the front. It is called *memory for context.* Example: "I just ran into her the other day, but *where?*

WHERE?" and it is among the most reliably unreliable kinds of episodic memory. For most of us, this one is a demon.

All this is normal. This is what tip-of-the-tongue-ness is all about. But what often sends people like ourselves into tailspins of worry is that (A) they do not know that it is normal and (B) it is the same kind of memory that goes first in *abnormal* conditions. So they sit ashen faced in waiting rooms, waiting to see the doctor: *I go to see a movie, and in a couple of days I can't even remember the name of the movie, and that is exactly what I saw happening with my uncle, and he had Alzheimer's, and, oh, my God, am I going to . . . ?*

Most probably not. Contrary to popular belief, Alzheimer's is *not* a strongly hereditary disease, as you'll find in Chapter Twelve, "So When *Isn't* It Normal?"

Also hanging off the declarative branch of this tree are *personal* and *impersonal episodic memory.* You are perhaps saying, "Enough with the tree," but stick with me here. Let me try to put it in emotionally resonant terms:

"The politician X has been found guilty of perjury, conspiracy, and fraud": that is impersonal episodic memory.

"Oh, boy, I just heard on the news that

the jury nailed X": that is personal episodic memory, and I, too, would say "Oh, boy."

There is also *prospective memory,* which some neurologists consider a separate system. In essence, it means memory for future events. Remembering to take your pills, to get money from the ATM, to show up for your lunch date — these all belong to prospective memory. It comes in two flavors: time based (remembering to take the pills a.m. and p.m.) and event based (remembering to repay the money that you owe a friend when the two of you meet for lunch).

Typically, we do much better with event-based memory than time-based, because of a handy little cognitive gadget called *priming:* the sight of the friend reminds you of the money.

Also in the declarative system: short-term and long-term memory.

To put these into basic (exceedingly basic) terms: An experience is transformed into a memory by a process called *encoding.* Let's return for the moment to that Olympic-scale nuisance of forgetting names. You meet Sally, you say, "Nice to meet you, Sally," you repeat silently, *Sally, Sally, Sally.*

Congratulations: Now you have encoded

the experience.

The next day, you see Sally on the street, and you can't remember her name. That is because you encoded it only superficially. It hung around for a minute or so in short-term memory, and then it was gone. Over and out.

To encode it more deeply, you would have needed to elaborate upon it, associate it in some way with things you already know, as I described earlier. Every memory that is encoded creates a different pattern of connections between neurons. The more you elaborate, the stronger the connections, the stronger the memory.

What the experts always stress about getting a memory into long-term storage is that what isn't being paid attention to cannot be stored. It is *gone.* And since paying attention, like multitasking, may become a bit more difficult with time, we need to pay more attention to paying attention.

As described in Chapter Five, paying attention is one of those so-called executive functions that are governed by the frontal lobe and may be improved by doing aerobics. (An activity to which, in itself, attention must be paid. As I sit here at my computer I am in less than perfect comfort, due to a cracked rib sustained a week ago, due to a fall off a treadmill, due to not paying attention to my feet. So, yes, it is good to exercise those frontal lobes. But watchfully.)

Short- and *long-term memory* are among the many phrases that I have always slung around without knowing exactly what they mean. How short is short-term? How long is long-term?

I took this one to Professor Stern, who cordially assured me that there *is* no exactly. "A minute or two would be *short,* and *long* might be days or weeks or years. But *very* short-term memory is a slightly different system."

"Ah. A separate branch of the tree?"

"Yes. We call it working memory. It's where things are first registered. It's sort of a scratch pad, like when you hang onto a telephone number until you punch it in — that's the scratch pad."

The elusive telephone number is the memory specialists' favorite example when they describe working memory. Which brings to mind a tidbit that you will perhaps be pleased to learn, as I was: It was the Cambridge University autism specialist Simon Baron-Cohen who told me that people on average can hang onto no more than seven digits at once — which is why we have seven-digit telephone numbers.

"The thing about working memory," Professor Stern said, "is that whatever comes into it has to be maintained, or it's gone. If you can maintain it sufficiently, it will be stored in declarative memory. And then, when you retrieve it from storage, it comes back to that scratch pad. That's the place where you use the information and manipulate it. It's sort of like what happens with your computer: You have documents that are stored on your hard drive, but when you want to work with one of them, it has to be retrieved from the hard drive into the working memory of the machine."

"Why would working memory and declarative memory be considered two separate systems?"

"Because they don't depend on the same areas of the brain. The systems are really all working together, but working memory primarily relies on different brain areas than long-term memory."

We come now to the third branch of the tree, which is called nondeclarative memory, or implicit memory. This is the kind that we use without being in the least bit conscious that we are using it.

Sensory memories — memory of a particular sound, a sight, a smell, and so forth — may be either conscious or unconscious, depending on how familiar they are.

For example, if you are a grilled-steak fancier and find yourself close to a steak broiling on an outdoor grill, you probably are not sniffing the air and wondering what that odor is. The recognition comes with no conscious awareness.

But if you pass by someone who is wearing, say, Chanel N° 5, a scent you happened to smell only once, long ago, and a whiff of the stuff hits the olfactory center of your brain, there is more likely to be a fully conscious response: *Where have I smelled this before? When? Upon whom?*

By contrast, true implicit memory is always unconscious. It sticks with us through practically any form of memory disorder, short of our becoming a total artichoke. It is also called *procedural memory:* virtually unforgettable, fully automatic, the kind we never think about.

Procedural memory is what Sinatra never thought about when he sang; what Astaire never thought about when he danced; what Tiger Woods does not think about when he swings his golf club. In fact, if he did think about it, it might very well ruin his stroke.

Procedural memory is what might be

called, in nontechnical terms, knowing-how memory. Knowing how to walk, to drink from a glass, to tie a shoe.

The procedural memory system develops early in life. One of the mysteries of memory is sometimes called childhood amnesia: Why it is that we don't remember much of anything that happened to us — the episodic memories — before age four or five? The rare individual may have sharp, clear memories from before that age, but most of us do not.

"Freud thought it was because, early on, there is trauma, and this trauma blocks the memory and it remains repressed in the unconscious, and all that stuff," I was told by the noted biological anthropologist Terrence Deacon, of the University of California, Berkeley, when we were talking about the evolution of memory. "But I think most people today doubt that. We really don't have the full component of memory systems until we are about between ages five and seven. I think what's going on before that age is, we're doing a lot of procedural memory building — learning language and skills and so forth.

"Those skills are becoming well developed and, in effect, biology doesn't want to have them disturbed by a lot of episodic memories at a time when the child doesn't have to deal with the episodic stuff.

"During childhood, if you're a mammal, you're taken care of. You don't need to go back and remember an episode of your life. Everything is being handed to you. That episodic system is not yet in demand, so to speak. When you really need it is when you begin to function more on your own, more autonomously. By then, the procedural memory system has been well established."

So procedural, in other words, is the first in and the last out. Episodic is the last in and, lamentably, the first out.

But think of it this way: It would be a whole lot worse the other way around.

Procedural memory is so deeply ingrained that it can even operate independent of the hippocampus, the brain's memory center, although cognitive researchers do not yet understand precisely how that works.

But I have seen it work. I once knew a woman who had been a musical prodigy, a brilliant pianist. At age sixteen she was giving concerts internationally. At age seventeen she had a severe schizophrenic breakdown. She was institutionalized for the next thirty years and repeatedly subjected to electric shock.

When she came out, and was housed by

relatives, she was still living pretty much in her own strange world, the zapping of her brain having left her weirdly affectless, and she had little memory for what had happened day before yesterday. But sit her down at a keyboard, and she made magic. The fingers remembered.

Procedural is what your fingers remember when you tie your shoelaces, what your feet remember when you ride a bike. Procedural, as my old friend, the late Helen Singer Kaplan, a well-known psychiatrist and sex therapist, used to say, is what your body remembers when you make love.

"That's the last thing to go," she announced once to a startled but consummately appreciative audience at my dinner table. "As long as you're physically healthy, you can be doing it when you no longer remember who you're doing it with."

Procedural memory, *olé!*

Chapter Eight:
Amnesia,
Hollywood Style
FORGET IT

A case history: Trudy, a successful shoe designer, was widowed at age fifty-seven in a sad and sudden way. Her husband of thirty-three years, flying home from a business meeting, was stricken by a coronary aboard the plane and was pronounced dead upon landing. I had never liked him much, but still. Sad and sudden.

Mourners came. Trudy received. A week passed, then two, and her children began urging her to return to work.

A month after her husband's death, Trudy went back to her office. Driving home, along the same fourteen-mile route that she had been taking twice a day, five days a week, for twenty-odd years, she was observed to be going at high speed. She hit a utility pole, suffered a broken shoulder, broken ribs, and various cuts and bruises, was briefly hospitalized, and then, again, found herself receiving at home.

The outpouring of sympathy was enormous. Everyone liked Trudy. Privately, friends shook their heads and raised all the obvious questions. How could it have been an accident? they asked each other. After all, she knew the route well enough to drive it blindfolded. Had she, in her grief, been trying to kill herself?

None of them knew that Trudy's husband had been psychologically abusive. None of them knew that Trudy had stayed in the marriage for . . . ah, whatever reasons people ever have for staying in unhappy marriages. None of them knew that, before departing on that trip, he had told her that he had a girlfriend and wanted a divorce. His death, however regrettable, was impeccable in its timing. It had saved her from the pain and humiliation of living in a country-club suburb as the rejected wife. Instead, she was the stoic, much-admired widow.

Some months later, she and I talked about it and I dared to ask: Had she been trying to do herself in?

"No!"

Then what had happened?

"I haven't any idea. I was just driving along and paying no attention. I was designing a shoe."

No tears for Trudy. She is happily remarried now, to a honey of a man, but that is not the issue. Here is the issue: If you put aside the emotional details, all that Sturm und Drang, and consider only *what happened,* then what happened to her is the kind of thing that has happened to most of us.

Try this on for size:

You are going from one familiar place to another. Walking, driving, bicycling — it doesn't matter how you go. You arrive. You look about, slightly befogged, surprised, as you realize that you have no conscious memory — none! — of having gone from point A to point B. *How did I get here? How long did it take me? Where was I, what was I doing, what was I seeing, what was I thinking in the interim?*

You were perhaps designing a shoe? In any event, thinking faraway thoughts, hopefully pleasant ones. Or possibly not thinking at all, not consciously, simply going along on automatic pilot because the route was utterly boring and routine and, really, you could get there, as everyone had said of Trudy, blindfolded.

Whatever the cause, you were not paying attention. *My mind,* we say, *was wandering,* as though the mind — as distinct from the brain — can pick itself up and go roaming off in its own direction. Which, in a sense, it can.

My friend, what you are experiencing in such moments is a form of amnesia. It can, and does, happen to anyone at any age. But it may happen more often when you are pushing fifty or sixty than when you are pushing twenty, because (A) it is no longer as easy to focus attention and (B) simply because the longer we have been following certain routines, and the more deeply familiar they have become — as that home-ward drive was for Trudy — the more likely we are to perform them with no conscious memory of performing them. We reach a point where it's automatic pilot all the way.

"It happens when you are only attending moment to moment and not trying to learn anything over the long run," says the Johns Hopkins cognitive neurologist Barry Gordon. "Say you're on the New Jersey Turn-pike, going from Baltimore to New York. How memorable is *that?*" (Answer: It is one of the most boring roads in the world. No offense, New Jersey.) "Even if it's not familiar, you're not taking it in. You don't need to. You just point your car in one direction and keep going.

"That's just the way I got to New York a couple of days ago. Then I walked from

Thirty-fifth Street to Forty-second Street, and I wouldn't be able to tell you what route I took. I had other things on my mind."

You might call this a normal amnesia, which only sounds contradictory. There is nothing remotely abnormal about it.

Let us consider the case of the legendary Massachusetts Institute of Technology scientist Norbert Wiener: essence of genius, essence of geek, essence of absentminded professor.

At MIT, they still tell — and tell and retell — Norbert Wiener stories. Such as the time he was chatting with a student in a school hallway, then asked, "Which way was I going when we met?"

"That way," said the student, pointing toward the cafeteria.

"Ah," said Wiener, "then I haven't had lunch yet."

Or the time his family moved to a new house near the old, and his wife, knowing her Norbert, gave him a note with the new address. But at day's end he remembered neither where he had put the note nor the new address, so he went to the old, and asked a child who was playing on the street, "Do you know where the Wieners moved to?"

"Yes, Daddy," she said. "Mommy sent me to bring you home."

Possibly apocryphal, though I hope not. (In later years, his daughter said that he had never failed to recognize her but that the rest was perfectly true.) There is something endearing about such off-the-wall absent-mindedness. We chuckle, knowing that as long as we have all our marbles — and Wiener, however eccentric he might have been, had all his — it could never happen to any of us.

But, in fact, the difference between the normal amnesia that many of us have experienced and the exotic obliviousness of Norbert Wiener is mainly one of degree. (Also, we may safely assume that his mind wandered at loftier altitudes than our own. The man invented cybernetics, whatever that is.)

Specialists speak of a *fugue* state, in which an amnesic may drift about with no knowledge of having suffered any memory loss — not even the loss of his or her own name. In his book *Searching for Memory,* the distinguished Harvard psychologist Daniel L. Schacter describes a case in which a soldier became traumatized during fighting in World War II. The man wandered in a blackout state with no awareness of who he was or where he was going, and, further, not even any *awareness* that he had no awareness, until, a month later, he came to his full senses in a hospital hundreds of miles away.

To me, there is a kind of fugue state, a minor variation upon this theme, in the experience of not being quite certain whether something really happened.

Recently I got a telephone call from a relative who lives in a distant city.

"Did you call me last night?" she said.

"No," I said. "What makes you ask?"

"Are you *sure* you didn't call?" Then she laughed. "Dumb question. Of course you'd remember." (Not a safe assumption.) "But it was so real. We had this whole conversation. I remembered it vividly when I got up this morning, but something about it felt weird and I asked one of the kids, 'Did you hear me talking to Martha last night?' He said no, and then I thought, Well, maybe I didn't talk to her. Maybe I dreamt it."

It has probably happened to you, too, this sort of confusion between the real and the imagined memory. It is common.

"Have you ever remembered something but felt unsure whether you dreamed it or whether it actually took place?" I ask a friend who happens to have an extraordinary memory in several languages.

"Of *course*," she says. "Hasn't everyone?"

Did I actually meet so-and-so on that street corner and have that conversation? Or did I dream it? It seems so real but I'm just not sure.

There is remembering, and then there is the *sensation* of remembering — two different processes. And sometimes that difference becomes fuzzy. It is akin to what happens when we are not certain whether we actually performed some task or merely thought to perform it. *Did I pay that bill, or did I simply think of doing it? Did I turn off the oven, or did I only think of turning it off?* — a confusion that has produced more than one scorched dinner in my time.

My husband insists that he has never experienced an interweaving of dream and reality. (Perhaps he has forgotten.) But when I ask if he ever has this other sensation, of confusing thought and deed, he says, "Are you kidding? It's an everyday occurrence! Did I take my pills, or did I just *think* about taking them?"

The pills, oh yes. You would not believe how much company you have in this business about the pills, including my own. (For my solution, and others, see Chapter Eleven.)

What I am calling normal amnesia is a

far, far stretch down the road from a clinical case, but the two have something crucial in common: The missing memory cannot be retrieved. It is not like the momentary block that we experience in those tip-of-the-tongue moments. The blocked item, that tidbit of information that is momentarily playing hide-and-seek with you, is *in* there. You know it is, because you are able to remember it later. But with amnesia, there is no block. It is an absence, a void.

In "pure" amnesia, meaning the kind caused by brain damage, the memory is absent because the region of the brain that should have locked it in cannot function. In "normal" amnesia, it is absent because we weren't paying attention. It is exactly as the memory researchers and memory therapists always stress: What is not recorded cannot be played back. What you do not pay attention to does not, cannot, will not get stored. Absent, nonexistent, missing in inaction.

Pure amnesia is rare, except in the movies. And in the movies, pure amnesia is usually pure baloney. If all your ideas about it are based on what you have seen in films, you have some very colorful but totally wrong ideas. ("No," says Dr. Gordon, speaking of all those B movies in which someone gets bopped on the head, loses his memory, gets bopped again and presto! memory is regained, "you do not get better from a second hit on the head. You stay the same or get worse.")

To get a fix on the differences between what happens in a clinical case of amnesia and what can so easily happen to any of us, let me briefly describe the real thing. It comes in two flavors: the pure kind, involving brain damage, technically known as *organic,* and the psychological kind, technically known as *functional.* (Actually, there is a third flavor: the consciously falsified kind, technically known as *faking.* Favored by people seeking to escape such infelicitous realities as debts, hanky-panky with the law, or the assorted bill-paying, lawn-mowing, mortgage-ridden yelps and yowls of daily life. To quote again that sly sage Publilius Syrus: "It is sometimes expedient to forget who we are.")

Pure amnesia may come from head injury or from stroke; from diseases such as encephalitis; or even, very rarely, anesthesia or extreme alcoholism. (For normal amnesia, a moderate amount of alcohol may do it. As it happens, I enjoy drinking but I am a poor drinker. It takes one martini or two glasses of wine to induce a moderate version of that state called alcoholic blackout, which means that in the morning I'll have big blanks about the night before.)

Pure amnesia can cause different kinds of memory loss, depending on what part of the brain has been damaged and in what degree. Its victims may lose memory of experiences prior to the injury (retrograde amnesia), or since the injury (anterograde amnesia), or some combination of both. But almost always, they remember who they are.

In functional amnesia, caused by psychological trauma, that may be exactly what they forget. As in that truly golden oldie, the Alfred Hitchcock thriller *Spellbound,* with Gregory Peck: Poor lug doesn't know who he is, thinks he committed a murder (Did he? *Gregory Peck?* Don't be silly), poses as a psychiatrist, falls for another psychiatrist (Ingrid Bergman), gets cured, suddenly remembers the big Who am I? fingers the true killer, clinch, and fade-out.

Forget it, folks. It is about as accurate as that other favorite movie device, drowning in quicksand.* The true functional amnesiac

* People do not drown in quicksand. People float in quicksand. Something to do with a law of physics: By the time you sink about halfway in, the muck will solidify, making it exceedingly hard to get out but near impossible to drown. Unless, of

is usually a lost soul wandering dazedly in the street, often looking like a homeless person, maybe wandering into a police station to ask for help.

Now let me set out a little scenario:

Suppose X was in a car accident ten months ago and suffered a head injury. Today he is walking past a drugstore near his home. This drugstore was robbed a year ago while he was making a purchase. Scary memory. As he walks by, he bumps into someone to whom he was introduced at a party yesterday.

If X is a victim of retrograde amnesia, he may remember the new acquaintance but not the robbery.

If he has anterograde amnesia, he may remember the robbery but not the new acquaintance.

If he has functional amnesia, he may remember neither the robbery nor the new acquaintance nor who he happens to be.

If he has normal amnesia, he remembers all the above, and may stop to chat with the new acquaintance and tell her about the robbery. But he probably can't remember what he was thinking about while driving to the drugstore from home, and quite pos-

---

course, you happen to fall in headfirst.

sibly can't remember where he parked the car.

And if, in addition, he can't remember the new acquaintance's name — that's us, folks!

For neuroscientists, amnesia can provide a kind of anatomy lesson of memory. By testing victims with brain-scanning techniques, they see which parts of the brain are activated, or fail to be activated, by various stimuli. In this way, they can learn more about which brain areas are essential to different kinds of memory. (FYI: Researchers speak of brain regions *lighting up* when they are activated, but it is not really so visually dramatic. What a brain scan actually shows is fluctuations in measurements such as oxygen and blood levels. When networks of neurons are telegraphing information to particular areas of the brain, more blood goes to those areas to handle the extra activity.)

There is the case, familiar to everyone who studies memory, of a man known as H.M. Back in the fifties, he had a large portion of his hippocampus surgically removed, to relieve him of devastating seizures. The surgery did the necessary, stopped the seizures, but in the process his short-term memory disappeared. His case contributed to scientific understanding of the role the hippocampus plays in everyone's memory.

As I write this, the man is still alive. Meet him somewhere and he may engage you in a wholly normal conversation and, ten minutes later, have no memory of ever having met you before. But he knows perfectly well who he is.

For me there is a special poignancy in this kind of amnesia because it recalls what happened to my late husband, Dr. Harold Lear.

After a major coronary, Hal had bypass surgery and emerged with his short-term memory shot to hell. I remember too well the night, a year later, when we attended a play at Lincoln Center in Manhattan. When we left the theater it was snowing, fat, furry, dazzling flakes. As we were crossing that grand plaza, he suddenly stopped and stood shaking his head, and I thought he was marveling at the beauty of the snowfall. But he was crying. "Oh, Martha," he wept. "What did we just see? I remember nothing about it. Nothing."

Though he had been greatly weakened physically by heart failure, the loss of memory pained him far more than any physical disability. But there was never any loss of his self-identity. It is, as Dr. Gordon says, the most unforgettable knowledge we have. In organic amnesia, you do not lose it short of becoming a total vegetable.

There is a gender factor to amnesia. The cognitive scientist with whom I discussed it did not want to be named — you cannot *imagine* the sensitivity of cognitive scientists to discussing gender factors — but he told me that most victims of functional amnesia are women. It is usually triggered by a very narrow range of very painful experiences: the death of a loved one, a desertion, a rape.

Faked amnesia is thought to be more common in men.

Traditionally, one big reason was to escape from a marriage. That was back in the days when the spouse who deserted was almost always the husband. The situation changed dramatically in the seventies, when many more wives began walking out and slamming the door behind them, and this change led me to ask the anonymous cognitive scientist, "Would it follow that proportionately more women might be faking amnesia these days, and more men suffering the real thing?"

He thought not. "The functional amnesiacs are still more often women. The sociopathic ones are more often men. But whether the causes are social or neurological, we just don't know."

(Not that women never fake it. Dr. Gordon has told me of the case of a woman who went missing for two years: "When she was found, she claimed to remember nothing about who she was or when or how she had disappeared from her previous life. But tracing backward, they found that she had left a note with instructions for food for the cat." Which is what I would call — forgive me — *really* letting the cat out of the bag.)

But as for us, for you and me and the kind of amnesia that sometimes afflicts us, and is more likely to afflict us as we get older, there is no gender factor whatever. Normal amnesia is an equal-opportunity employer.

Think back to the last time you could not reconstruct some achingly familiar task that you performed in your morning ablutions or in your daily exercise routine or while boiling potatoes in your kitchen. Or on your trip, say, from the office to your home.

Somebody asks, "Do they still have that closed lane on the highway?"

You say, "I don't know."

"You *don't know?* You were just there. How can you not know?"

"Amnesia."

May all our afflictions be so benign.

CHAPTER NINE:
TELLING IT LIKE IT
ISN'T

MEMORY AND ITS DECEPTIONS

It is an amazement, the billions of memories that dwell in that three-pound organ (roughly; your brain is about two percent of your body weight) tucked into our skulls, and our ability to retrieve, out of those billions, a single memory of something that happened a day, a year, a decade ago. Truly an amazement. And yet, despite all that, it cannot be said that memory is the most reliable commodity that ever came down the pike.

Case in point: One recent evening I was with two old friends, the film critic Molly Haskell and the television correspondent Betty Rollin, who have known each other since they were fresh out of college.

The talk turned, as talk in our circles often does these days, to back pain — whether Betty's or Molly's or mine I do not remember, but the subject was back pain. Effortlessly and inevitably as spring into summer, this segued into a discussion of arthritis, cholesterol, and, of course, the vagaries of memory.

I said, "Isn't it amazing how, all of a sudden, we're always talking about health?"

Molly said, "When I was growing up, I used to hear my mother and her friends talking on and on about their health all the time, and I swore that I would never be like that. But I didn't realize how much *fun* it would be."

Betty said, "That's my line."

Pardon?

" 'How much *fun* it would be.' That's what *I* said, years ago, about *my* mother and her friends."

The question has not been resolved, and doubtless never will be. Each remains utterly convinced that it was her line.

Telling it like it wasn't. It happens all the time. It happens more easily as we get older, for reasons that we will come to soon. But first let us consider *deliberate* misattribution, of which we are currently seeing a lot.

This first decade of the new century has been rich in noted liars and plagiarists. Not that there was ever a shortage of them, but now we have the mixed blessing of the Web. It makes cheating so much easier. Computer buffs can surf around, lift a little bit of this and a little bit of that, and plaster their own names on top of other people's work. If caught, they often plead innocence: I confused sources. I forgot. It's not *me,* folks, it's my memory.

Polls show that huge numbers of college students do it and defend it. Could it be — just a suggestion — that they value truth less because truth has been so devalued in our culture, from the very top down? (Recall, if you can bear to: "I did not have sexual relations with that woman." "There is no doubt that Saddam Hussein has weapons of mass destruction." In politics, flimflam has no party affiliation.)

There was that brouhaha, in 2006, over the Harvard student who wrote a novel that the literary critics went gaga for, until they learned that she had copied many of its passages verbatim from somebody else's novel. When she was caught, she said that it was an honest error, caused by her own "photographic memory."

There was that bozo memoirist in the same year, consciously inventing phoney-baloney, passing it off as his own true life story — big, *big* best seller — and finally being given what-for on the *Oprah Winfrey Show.*

We are dealing here with two different

kinds of liar: a plagiarist and a fabulist. It has been said that the difference between them is that plagiarists steal because they suspect that their own talents aren't good enough, whereas fabulists lie because they suspect that their own truths aren't interesting enough. I trust their suspicions.

But then we have cases of people whose own talents are plenty good enough, yet they still get tarred with the brush of plagiarism.

Think of the flap over Bob Dylan. That was a juicy one. "Who's This Guy Dylan Who's Borrowing Lines from Henry Timrod?" gleefully asked one newspaper headline, Timrod being a little-known Civil War poet from whom Dylan seemed to have borrowed liberally in an album whose credit line read "All songs written by Bob Dylan." Oh, my aching heart.

Think of the historians Doris Kearns Goodwin and the late Stephen Ambrose, both having been accused several years back of borrowing from others — she in her book *The Fitzgeralds and the Kennedys* and he in *The Wild Blue,* and possibly other of his titles as well.

Both at the top of their game, both with everything to lose by claiming other people's stuff, and both surely aware how pathetically easy it is, these days, to be found out. So what was going on? The question that comes to mind is the one that NBC's Jay Leno put to the English actor Hugh Grant, after Grant was arrested for being serviced by a street hooker in a car that was parked, mind you, not in some remote dense wood, but just off Sunset Strip in Los Angeles. Cameras rolling, Leno asked, "What the hell were you thinking?"

Exactly.

Dismissing (though I don't, completely) the two-penny Freudian theory that people who do such things may unconsciously *want* to be caught, let's consider other possibilities.

Ambrose defiantly kissed off all critics: "If I am writing up a passage, and it is a story I want to tell and this story fits and a part of it is from other people's writing, I just type it up that way and put it in a footnote." Sort of a *droit du seigneur.*

Goodwin apologized. The trouble, she said, had been in careless note taking; she hadn't properly marked her sources in some nine hundred pages of hand-written notes.

That *is* careless. It is also a quaint way to preserve research material. But might Goodwin have made an honest mistake?

She might. In such cases, I would just as

soon assume so. First, because it costs no more. Second, because, beyond doubt, unintentional plagiarism exists. There is even a word for it: *cryptomnesia.* Terrific word. You may know it. I did not, until I found it in my trusty Webster's: "Cryptomnesia: the appearance in consciousness of memory images which are not recognized as such but which appear as original creations."

In other words, if you make use of somebody else's mental property and claim it as your own because you truly fail to remember that it is *not* your own, that is cryptomnesia. You are a cryptomnesiac. (Oh, I *do* love that word.) It happens routinely in certain professions. Songwriters and screenwriters, for example, who often work in teams, can no longer remember who wrote what and often take credit for each other's lines.

I know how easy it is to do, because I myself have done it, in a way.

Once I wrote an article about marital therapy for *The New York Times Magazine.* A reader sent a letter to the editor crying, *plagiarism!* He remembered reading remarkably similar words long before, although he didn't recall the source.

He was right. I *had* plagiarized — from

myself. (Autocryptomnesia?) I had totally forgotten that I had expressed some of the same views, on the same subject, in the same publication, almost two decades earlier, when marital therapy, along with sex therapy and a pipe dream called Open Marriage, had been hugely in vogue. But *something* must have kicked in, unconsciously, when I wrote that second article.

That something may have been related to the phenomenon I mentioned earlier, called priming, the unconscious cueing of memory. For instance: Repeatedly given a puzzle to solve, a victim of amnesia will solve it with greater ease each time — with no conscious memory of ever having encountered the puzzle before.

Well, then: Doesn't this make it possible that, as we become increasingly familiar with someone else's mental property — an idea, an anecdote, an experiment, an invention, a joke, a text, a recipe, a you name it — doesn't this make it possible that we might begin, in all good faith, to take it as our own?

In his book *Searching for Memory,* the Harvard psychologist Daniel L. Schacter writes: "Experiments have shown that simply repeating a false statement over and over leads people to believe that it is true. Likewise, when we repeatedly think or talk about a past experience, we tend to become increasingly confident that we are recalling it accurately."

And from middle age on, it becomes increasingly likely to happen. Not simply because of all the general effects of time — how time blurs memory of an event or solidifies false versions of the event — but more specifically, because, as I've noted before, *source memory,* memory for context ("I just heard that story, but from *whom?*" "I ran into them recently, but *where?*") is one of the first kinds of memory to begin giving us the runaround. Which can be extremely scary, although — and here I repeat myself with pleasure — it is totally normal.

Add to this the ever-present tip-of-the-tongue problem: that precisely right adjective that is just beyond your reach. You may remember the event well enough but be unable to find the words to describe it accurately — and the spoken description then becomes the version of record.

Then, too, since memories, like dreams, are affected by unconscious desires and fears, the way we remember is profoundly colored by the familiar coulda woulda shoulda. We are always dealing with (A) the event as it actually happened, overlaid by (B) how we think it *might* have happened, further modified by (C) how we may believe that it *should* have happened, and additionally burdened by (D) how we *wish* that it had happened or (E) how we *fear* that it actually happened.

That is a lot of weight to throw on a memory. No wonder the poor thing sometimes lists slightly to the left or the right of accuracy. And each time that you retrieve it, of course, it then goes back into storage, and in the process may be further altered. Which is what happens when you think you remember perfectly some experience from early childhood. What you are probably retrieving is the version you most recently deposited back into those hidden depths of the memory bank — perhaps further distorted by parents' and siblings' memories of the same event.

A dear friend who was born in Greece — Domna Stanton, a professor of French literature — has Technicolor memories of certain childhood experiences there. "But I don't have a clue whether I remember those things as they actually happened to me, or as the family kept retelling those stories over the years. I can't even be sure that they happened at all, even though I remember them so vividly."

And then there are the distorting effects of guilt. Guilt is a miserable roommate. It inspires us to edit our memories into versions that we can live with. The older we get, the more editing we do and the less we believe that we have done any editing at all.

A psychotherapist tells me of two such rewritten narratives:

A patient was forty-six when his father died. He had had a difficult relationship with both his parents, had not spoken to his father for several years, and did not attend the funeral.

His mother could not forgive him. He could not forgive himself. Over the years he moved from convincing himself that (A) he had been justified in not going to the funeral to (B) he would have gone but knew that his father would not have wanted him to be at the funeral to (C) he had actively wanted to go, but his mother had suggested that he would not be welcome at the funeral. He died at the same age — sixty-eight — as his father, on the same date as his father, believing C absolutely.

The therapist had another patient (also dead now; she would never discuss a case history in a patient's lifetime), who was babysitting his preschool grandchild when a fire broke out in a nearby building. He wanted to see the fire, so he took the child. There were frightening scenes, including a body being carried from the building, that left the child with night terrors for months. The patient's guilt — over having allowed his grandchild to witness this scene, with all the trauma that followed — was more than he could handle. And so he rewrote the narrative, simply by editing the child out of the story: He had gone to the scene alone. He had gone there briefly, just to make sure that the fire was not spreading. So he said and so he believed, insisting that the child had imagined being with him; and so he went on believing until finally he was led by the therapist, dragging his heels all the way, to a confrontation with the truth.

I think, actually, that there is another way in which age affects all these self-deceptions. We are told — I don't know by whom, exactly, but we keep getting told — that we become mellower as we get older. I don't believe it for a moment. I believe, as I've said before, that what we become as we get older is more of whatever we were to begin with.

"This grandfather — was he always the kind of person who can't say, 'I made a mistake'?" I asked the therapist.

"Oh, was he ever!" she said.

So that is editing memory for reasons of guilt, and we all do it, though hopefully in less baroque ways.

Then we come to embroidering memory for reasons of . . . well, for reasons of wanting to win friends, influence people, and get invited to swell parties.

We like to tell a good story. A good story makes for a popular dinner guest. And being as morally frail as the next humanoid, we may tell that story a little bit taller every time we tell it. It is the quintessential fish that got away. Do we, in time, come to believe it? Need you ask? Repeat it often enough, and you'll end up swearing to its accuracy in the witness box with your hand on your grandmother's Bible.

Now add all the ways in which memory can get bent by the power of suggestion, which could be, and has been, a book (many books) in itself. You need only think back to the nineties, to all those cases of preschoolers persuaded that they had been sexually abused by their nursery-school teachers, duly followed by an outbreak of "recovered memory" cases — young women who suddenly recalled being sexually abused by their fathers when they were children. It was contagious. It spread to epidemic proportions. And then, quite suddenly — *pfft.* Wherever did all those epidemics go?

In fact, some psychiatrists and cognitive scientists do not believe at all in the Freudian concept of repressed memory, dear as it is to the hearts of Hollywood producers. The debate raged through the nineties, then died down, then flared up again with the charges of sexual abuse against Catholic priests. Some nonbelievers say that a memory is not actively repressed but is simply forgotten, that it sits around in the overcrowded depths of the brain doing nothing whatever for years, for decades, until something cues it.

Add to all these influences upon memory the further distorting effects of pride and ego — the long, self-protective reach of the ego.

Try this: A couple gets married. Everybody's happy. You say, "There's a marriage I bet will last forever."

Five years later comes the divorce. You say (well, perhaps not you, but *I* might), "I always suspected it wouldn't last" — and that is what you believe.

If a friend helpfully notes, "Remember when you said that it would last forever?"

you say, "No, that wasn't what I said!" — and you believe that, too.

It is not just the effects of time and age. The need to feel *right* is a huge factor in how we remember and how we forget. The twin bookends of ego protection: "I never said that!" and "I always knew it!"

In Joan Didion's brilliant book *The Year of Magical Thinking,* she describes the high-wire act of trying to persuade reluctant doctors, without antagonizing them, to try a particular treatment on her critically ill daughter: "There was a way to know if you had made headway. You knew you had made headway when a doctor to whom you had made one or another suggestion presented, a day later, the plan as his own."

Yet that doctor might — there is no way to know, but he *might* — have convinced himself that the plan was his own. Especially since doctors, perhaps beyond all others, have a need to feel *right.*

An architect friend, who used to live and work in a resort town, recalls with under-standable indignation the time a well-known, well-heeled couple asked her to design a ski house for them:

I saw an ad for these beautiful old tim-bers from eighteenth-century English barns. I thought, "Wouldn't it be great to reassemble them in the field! It wouldn't be structural, obviously, but it would be a wonderful exterior."

My clients loved the idea. So I did it, and it worked out marvelously. They were thrilled. And a year later we were all sitting in a restaurant, and the wife was talking about how much she loved the house, and she said, "Thank heaven I had that idea for the English barn."

I was totally dumbstruck. She couldn't really have believed that, could she?

She could. I'm not saying that she did, but she could. And as time passes, and she and the timbers both continue to age, she doubtless grows more secure in her belief.

Again, it's the triumph of ego over memory. Happens all the time.

Forgetting is often pure tactic. Maybe conscious, maybe unconscious, but always deliberate. And sometimes extremely hard to read — a well-mixed psychological bag.

I witnessed the breakup of a long, close friendship between two women I've known for years. Call them Jane and Mary. The trouble involved money, which almost always means trouble. Jane needed money and Mary loaned it to her. It was a modest amount, but still. A loan. And months went by and no mention of the loan. And Jane bought a new computer but no mention of the loan. And Jane took a trip to the Galápagos Islands but no mention of the loan. And Mary grew more and more resentful.

"When someone says 'It's not about the money,' you know it's about the money." An old saw, smart and funny and often accurate. But in this case, it really was not about the money. It was about Mary's feeling of being used — not a feeling that many of us can handle with grace.

She told me, "I promised myself that I would be classy enough never to raise the subject. Then I raised it. She said, 'I forgot.' And she looked angry. And two days later the check arrived, and that was the end of the friendship."

Had Jane forgotten? *Sort of* forgotten? Felt a fully conscious sense of entitlement: "I needed it and you had it and therefore you have no right to expect it back"?

No way to know. But you may be certain that it was, on some murky level of motive, a tactic.

Sometimes the tactic is blatantly conscious. Example: people who never remember who you are, no matter how many times you've met. I know an actress, no big star but splendid at her craft, whose ears spew smoke whenever the name of another actress (far better known, not nearly as talented) is mentioned.

"That phony," she tells me. "I've met that woman again and again and it's always the same thing — 'Oh, how do you do' — you know, as though we never met before. I always feel like telling her, 'Listen, you and I have met a thousand times before. Are you having a *senior moment?*' "

"Why don't you?" I ask.

She shrugs. "Scared of what she might say."

"Like what?"

"Like, 'You're just not memorable.' "

(If you are in the market for counterattack strategies, another woman I know has an effective one. She strikes before the repeat offender can hit her with the same old How do you do. The offender's name is, say, Dorothy. "Daphne!" my friend says brightly. "How nice to see you, Daphne!" And smiles warmly and ambles off. I've seen her do it. Smooth.)

Fully (one hopes) unaware, we all manage to play tactical tricks on our own memories all the time. You keep forgetting to make an obligatory telephone call or write a difficult condolence note or run an unpleasant errand. You promise reluctantly to do a favor and never remember to do it. You accept a dinner invitation under duress and forget to go. (Especially likely to happen when the host, instead of saying, "Can you come to dinner on the fifteenth?" says, "When can you come to dinner?")

"Happens constantly," says the New York City psychologist Margaret Sewell. "I had a patient who forgot an appointment because she resented my changing a previous appointment. It was quite out of her consciousness, very different from saying, 'Screw Sewell, I'll stand her up, she jerked me around.' That also happens, of course. But when I called her, she said, 'Oh, my God, I had an appointment? I'm so *sorry*' . . . rather than coming in and saying to me, 'I was so pissed at you,' which would have been too difficult for her to do, because this is someone who is uncomfortable being angry with people.

"So forgetting can be a seemingly benign occurrence that is loaded with feelings that are uncomfortable for the person who is doing the forgetting. You forget someone's birthday because you're angry with them, or disappointed in them, or because they didn't remember your birthday . . . the reason behind such forgetting usually being that those feelings are unacceptable to you."

I've had it both ways: forgotten other people's birthdays and been forgotten in turn. Forgotten, with clear conscience, to show up at other people's homes, and been angry when they forgot to show up at mine. Which brings me straight to what is (if memory serves me correctly) the worst memory lapse of my life. Today, more than two decades later, I still shrink into my skin to recall it.

I was to host a birthday party. The birthday boy was the late Sey Chassler, the editor of *Redbook* magazine, a fine editor and a good friend for whom I had written many articles over the years. It was a major birthday — naturally, I don't remember which one, but it was major — and I said that I would like to give a celebratory dinner for him, and we put together a guest list of twelve.

The big night arrived. The guests arrived.

Alas. The hostess was out for the evening.

I had put it down in my calendar for the following week.

When I got home, a note was waiting in the lobby of my apartment building. It said, "We were here. Where were you?" followed by eleven signatures.

I wanted to slit my throat.

The birthday boy most generously forgave me. (Also, most generously, after the group had been milling around in the lobby for a time, trying to figure out what to do, he had taken them all out to a Chinese restaurant for dinner.) But I never forgave myself. And I never understood it. This was a party I had *wanted* to give, this was a friend I treasured. Why I had managed so royally to screw it up, I will never know — and devoutly do not want to know.

Unless, of course, it was one of those occasions — they do occur — when a cigar is truly just a cigar. Wrong calendar entry, period.

Which I bring up here to illustrate that, amid all these devious tricks of the mind, we nonetheless ought to be on guard lest we overinterpret. To wit: My late husband's mother was in a convalescent home following a stroke. Each time we visited, Hal would ask her what we could bring the next time. Once she said, "Bring me my wedding dress."

"Your what?"

"My wedding dress, my *wedding* dress." Impatiently, as if to say What's the problem?

We waited to one side while a nurse gave her pills. Hal looked stricken. "I guess this is it," he muttered.

But no, that was *not* it. His mother's memory was fine. It turned out that another patient in the convalescent home was going to have an anniversary party the following week, and she did indeed want her wedding dress — her *party* dress, the one that she had always worn to weddings.

From which I learned an invaluable lesson: Just because it looks like a duck and walks like a duck and quacks like a duck, make no assumptions. Not when the subject is memory.

CHAPTER TEN: OUCH! THAT HURTS TO REMEMBER

I have a lot of arthritis in my left hand and wrist. It doesn't hurt all the time, but when it does, it hurts like the devil.

When it does *not* hurt, I cannot accurately recall the pain. I can *describe* it. I can point to the enlarged knuckle of my thumb and say, "Sometimes it feels like a nail being driven in." I can encircle my wrist and say, "Sometimes it feels as though someone is twisting it off." But those, as I say, are mere descriptions of sensations. What I cannot do is retrieve the actual sensations as they feel in full bloom.

Nor can I retrieve the pain of a recent, exceedingly bad toothache or the pain that made me double up when I had a fibroid tumor flopping around in my gut, or whatever. And how very nice that I can't.

We simply cannot retrieve with precision the experience of physical pain. (Nor can we do it with physical pleasure. Try calling up the precise sensation of a sexual climax. You can't, really — which is just as well because if you could, no one would ever get any work done. Mother Nature was no dummy.)

"There is no literal memory of pain," Cornell's Dr. Relkin says. "You can remember *being* in pain, but if you try to resurrect the image of pain that you had at root canal, or childbirth, you can't bring that up. Pain does not have that kind of representation in our memory."

Now here's the oddity: We can call up *emotional* pain very well indeed. Moments of remorse or humiliation, the agonies of rejection or failure or grief — we can retrieve them with great accuracy.

By "retrieve with great accuracy," I mean much more than the act of remembering. I mean the actual reexperiencing of the sensation. Grief especially. The phenomenon of memory is astonishing in so many ways, and here is one of them, that memory can do this: that months, years, even decades after the death of a loved one, we may suddenly be reminded of the beloved by a face quickly glimpsed in the street or a fragrance or a brief drift of melody, and feel a stab of pain fully as sharp as when the loss was new. It doesn't take much of a cue to stir the memory bank.

A personal story here, if I may, to illustrate the point. It was awful when it happened, but it had a happy ending. It has to do again with my late husband, the urologist Harold Lear, about whose odyssey of illness and subsequent death I wrote in a book called *Heartsounds.* Undeniably, we do idealize the dear departed, just as we demonize others. Have you noticed how all ex-wives are crazy, all ex-husbands are bastards, and all dead spouses are saints? But this one really was a splendid man, and I adored him, and his death at age fifty-eight was the most painful event of my life. I had a long, tough time getting over it.

Once, three years after he died, I was walking down some street and suddenly saw, just in profile, a man who looked like Hal, who walked with Hal's stride, and *wham.* It took all I had to restrain myself from racing across the street and clutching at the stranger's sleeve. (The impulse cannot always be restrained. A friend told me recently of a similar experience. She saw a young man in the street who was "a dead ringer," she said, for the beloved brother who had been killed in Vietnam at age nineteen. She ran to him and grabbed him and stood there, almost four decades after the fact, sobbing on the startled boy's shoulder. "Imagine it!" she said. I certainly could. I think anyone who has lost a loved one can imagine it.)

Fast-forward to an evening, years after I was widowed, when friends invited me to a small dinner party. Among the guests was an attractive man who appeared to be alone. I thought perhaps the hosts were trying to match-make, but it was no such thing. One of them took me aside and told me that they had asked him to dinner in hopes of lifting his spirits. He had been a "basket case" since the recent loss of his wife. I heard that word *recent,* and I thought, *Poor man; I remember.*

At the dinner table, everything was pleasant small talk until someone asked him how long ago his wife had died. In the sudden silence, I heard him say, "Eight months ago."

Again, *wham.* Courtesy of our memories, we are all — sometimes wondrously, sometimes painfully — human time machines. I heard "Eight months ago," and instantly I was transported back through time and space to when I had been just eight months widowed, to how it had felt to be just eight months widowed. I felt it precisely, the same old pain seeped like sludge into my bones, I was *there*. To everyone's astonishment, especially mine, I began to cry — not decorously, but in the loud, pungent way that makes people wish you'd go elsewhere and blow your nose. Which I did. Mumbled apologies and fled to another room, feeling humiliated.

He came after me. It stunned me (and still does) that this man, who bore such grief of his own, should come to comfort *me*. But loss and grief are an enormity to have in common. It enabled us to cut through the tiresome rituals of Getting to Know You. We quickly became friends, and then more than friends, and then consolidated our households, and in time we were married.

None of which, I have always been convinced, would have happened without the cue, "eight months ago," which caused a particular memory of emotional pain to come surging out of wherever in my brain it happened to be stored and to be retrieved, wide-screen and in living color.

Now why should the agony of a major toothache not be recalled with the same precision?

Come back to Mother Nature: If you take the Darwinian view of how things work, as do most of the scientists whom I have interviewed, there is probably a reason.

These distinctions didn't just happen to happen. They must have been, as the Darwinists say, somehow adaptive — offering some sort of evolutionary advantage.

Back in the late eighties, I was a regular contributor to a column called "Body and Mind," in *The New York Times Magazine.* One of my columns was titled "Designs in Nature." It was about nature's own balancing act, burdening us in modern life with problems that once, well back before recorded time, may have served some adaptive purpose — a kind of primordial buy now, pay later plan.

A case dramatically in point was the medically well-established and curious fact that heart attacks tend, beyond numerical probability, to happen in the morning hours. Why might this be?

Here was the theory of Dr. Louis Teichholz, who was then associate chief of cardiology at the Mount Sinai Medical Center in New York:

"Think of prehistoric man going forth to hunt. When would he have done this? Most likely in the morning, when he woke up. He would have wanted, speaking teleologically, to have plenty of adrenaline in the morning so that he would perform well in the hunt. And adrenaline makes the blood thicker, stickier, more clotable. His blood would have *wanted* to be thicker in the morning so that, if he got cut by a stone or clawed by an animal, he wouldn't bleed to death. And that may be why we have more adrenaline in the morning, which is why heart attacks are more likely to happen in the morning. Teleologically speaking, of course."

(Teleology: "the philosophical study of evidences of design in nature. The use of design, purpose, or utility as an explanation of any natural phenomenon." — Webster's)

In the same column, Dr. George F. Cahill, Jr., a specialist in metabolic disease who was then a vice president of the Howard Hughes Medical Institute in Bethesda, Maryland, proposed a teleological explanation for many autoimmune diseases, such as type I diabetes, multiple sclerosis, and myasthenia gravis, all of which have high occurrence in northern European countries.

"As waves of population from the Near East moved northward across Europe four thousand years ago, they huddled together against the cold and developed highly infectious diseases — probably tuberculosis and syphilis," Dr. Cahill said. "Out of this came a more vigorous immune-response system, surviving with the people who survived. And today their descendants have too much of a good thing. The very vigor of these immune systems may cause autoimmune reactions, and so we find this high incidence of autoimmune diseases in northern Europe."

He offered also a neat — not comforting to hear, perhaps, but neat — explanation for middle-age bulge: "In primitive times, when the life span was so short, there may have been a selective advantage to keeping some of the older population fattened up for survival. After all, there was no recorded history. People had to rely on memory. You would have wanted to keep a few fat old people around so someone could remember where the old watering hole was. And that may be why we lose caloric regulation in our later decades."

I love such speculations. And because they are, of course, well beyond proof (or disproof, for that matter), another theory of fat, as offered to me by Dr. Jeffrey S. Flier, then specializing in diabetes and metabolism at Beth Israel Hospital in Boston, serves just as well.

Suggesting why our metabolism tends to get sluggish in our later decades, he said of prehistoric man:

"As you got older, perhaps you got less useful as a hunter-gatherer, and you'd be waiting back at camp for leftover food. And it might be a long wait. So there would be a reason to have a metabolism that would permit more caloric storage . . . The kind of metabolism people wish they had today — where, despite the engorgement of large amounts of disgustingly rich food, they remain lean — that metabolism would not have been useful when you managed to eat a good meal *maybe* once a week.

"Those people would have been the first to die in times of famine. The people who are always starving themselves and complaining, 'Any little thing I eat, I gain weight' — they would have had the optimal advantage. The genes that survive are those that *on balance* provide some adaptation. After a period of starvation, the genes for inefficient metabolism might be lost and those for thrifty metabolism — that which gets the greatest bang for the buck — would survive."

Those genes that *on balance* provide some adaptation. Now come back to that emotional pain that is so hard to forget and that physical pain that is so hard to remember. What could be the on-balance advantage of *that?*

Well, most of us can meet the basic responsibilities of our lives, even when we're feeling emotional pain. You catch sight of a former boss who humiliated you, or a former friend who betrayed you, and suddenly find yourself seething with the same old impotent rage. You watch a television drama in which somebody's mother dies, and suddenly you are flooded with grief for the loss of your own long-gone mother, as if it had happened yesterday. But you can manage, when you must, to get it together and tend to the family, go to the office, do the job, put a meal on the table, pay the bills, get done whatever it is that needs to be done.

Imagine, though, if every minor twinge in your viscera caused you not simply to remember but literally to relive some terrible postsurgical pain. Or if seeing someone toting a broken arm in a sling made you cry out with the agony of a fracture that you suffered long ago.

Or think of that prehistoric hunter in Dr. Teichholz's scenario: Suppose, every time he picked up his weapon to go forth and hunt, he suddenly reexperienced the pain of being clawed by his prey. Would he still go forth? Or would he say, "Sorry, guys, I pass, let someone else bring home the bacon"?

If we had literal memory of great physical pain, we might become immobilized. Society might cease to function in an orderly way. And if you consider the classic example, the pains of childbirth, we might have a spectacular downturn in population growth and even possibly, as a species, do a slow fade.

Childbirth: You go through it and you swear you will never forget it and then you pretty much do forget it. Suppose you didn't?

"You know, it's that old thing about women and all the pain of giving birth," Dr. Yaakov Stern says. "If they could remember how painful it was, maybe they wouldn't do it anymore."

As I say, Mother Nature was no dummy. Teleologically speaking, of course.

CHAPTER ELEVEN:
THE MED STUDENT
SYNDROME

THIS MUST BE ALZHEIMER'S

Probably the best way to explain the Med Student Syndrome, which does not roll off the tongue as trippingly as Social Anxiety Syndrome and other inspired inventions of the pharmaceutical industry, is to tell you about my conversation last year with Jessica Hoover, a first-year student at Johns Hopkins School of Medicine.

"I remember it vividly," said Jessica, who was then twenty-three. At that age they remember everything vividly. "We were having a lecture on skin. We were seeing blow-ups of normal skin compared to abnormal. And suddenly I was looking at this huge blowup of a patch of skin with two dark spots and one kind of pinkish lesion. Well, I was a lifeguard for years, and I have moles like that on my chest, and I thought, 'Oh, my God, that's *me.*'

"I called my mother, who is a pathologist, and I said, 'Mom, I think I have melanoma.'

And she said, 'Jehhhs . . . ,' in that tone of voice, you know, like, Oh, here we go again. 'Jehhhs, you do not have melanoma. In med school you are going to think you have every disease you're learning about. When you learn about brain tumors, you'll get headaches. When you learn about the physiology of the heart, you'll get palpitations. When you learn about the digestive system, you'll get stomachaches and diarrhea.' "

That is the Med Student Syndrome.

I asked the neurologist Barry Gordon, who was one of Jessica's professors, if he himself had ever suffered the syndrome.

"Oh, sure. It's usually the mole issue: *Has this changed? What is it?* And it's not just students. When I was an intern I used to do a lot of push-ups in bare feet, and that puts a lot of pressure on your big toes. I developed a black spot on my toe, and I was really worried that it was a melanoma. I went to a dermatologist and she said, 'It's nothing.' I said, 'How can you be sure?' She said, 'Okay, if I can't convince you, why don't we just cut off your toe?' I did insist on a biopsy, and, of course, it was nothing."

I tell you this not out of any consuming interest in mole issues, but because from the Med Student Syndrome it is just a nervous hop and a skip to the This Must Be

Alzheimer's Syndrome (not pharmaceutically inspired, although the drug houses may yet figure out some way to market it).

It seems that most everyone I know, from early middle age upward, has at one point or another whacked the side of her or his head with an open palm, said to me, "I don't remember *anything* anymore," and then, with that characteristically mirthless chuckle, made some reference to Alzheimer's disease.

This has caused a certain adjustment in my thinking. Enjoying, as I do, an occasional day at the races, I always used to assume that when anyone said "the Big A," they meant Aqueduct, the New York City racetrack.

Not anymore.

Forgot where you left your eyeglasses (keys, wallet, whatever)? "I think I'm getting Alzheimer's."

Forgot to return a phone call, pay a bill, bring things to the cleaner's? "I must be getting Alzheimer's."

Forgot to show up for a lunch date? "I swear I'm getting Alzheimer's."

"Not that I really mean it," a friend says, in a semi-disclaimer typical of many I hear, "but I say it anyway. We all say it, and we all know that we can't *all* be getting Alzheimer's. But when I think of something I have to do, and three seconds later I can't remember what it was — that drives me crazy. That's one unpleasant result of not remembering things: I'm continuously angry at myself."

"But you're laughing. Why?"

She thinks a moment. "Well, I suppose the laugh is discomfort, but it's also comfort, because everyone I mention it to has the same complaints. So it's 'Oh, you too!' It would be awful if you were the only one. But there's something sort of funny about all of us being in the same boat."

I get an e-mail: "Can't remember if I sent you a reminder (that's my problem in a nutshell). See you tonight at 7:30." The sender is Letty Cottin Pogrebin, author, activist on many fronts, and one of the busiest people I know. She didn't used to have to send reminders asking if she had sent a reminder. But . . . join the club. It is everyone's problem in a nutshell.

At a dinner party, I find myself sitting next to a high-level executive with one of the largest bookstore chains in the country. He is telling me about a book he is reading. The subject is the history of obituaries. "It sounds dreary, but it's really fascinating and great fun to read," he says.

"What's the title?"

"I can't remember." He pauses. We are brand-new acquaintances, I do not expect confidences. Then he says: "You know, I'm fifty-seven years old. I'm just at the edge, that boomer edge. There are so many of us!" (FYI: Sociologists generally define the baby-boom years as from 1946 to 1964, an astonishingly fecund postwar period in which there were *seventy-eight million* births.) "And I worry about this all the time. I meet you tonight and we talk and tomorrow I can't remember your name. I'm telling you about this book I'm reading and I can't even remember the title. My friends and I kid about it all the time. It's happening to all of us and the reason we kid about it is because we're worried. 'Am I getting Alzheimer's? Do I have anything to worry about?' And what I want to know is, should I be worried, or is it normal? Because if it's normal, I won't worry about it."

He *looks* worried. Worry sits on him like a suit. I feel like wrapping my arms about him, as one might a child who is scared of starting school, and saying, "There, there, cookie, it's normal."

Every memory therapist can tell you stories of the hard drivers and high achievers coming to them in distress and in droves, because they can't remember this and they can't remember that and "Doctor, could this be Alzheimer's?"

The "Worried Well," the psychiatrist Gayatri Devi calls them.

The Worried Well. Hello, are you there?

For the Worried Well, the syndromes du jour used to be heart attacks and breast cancer. I think back to how things were in the eighties, when I had written in the book *Heartsounds* about my late husband's first coronary:

> To be American, male, in one's fifties, a compulsive worker — as who of them is not? — worried about cholesterol and unpaid bills, working under stress and watching old friends succumb, one by one, to that crisis of the heart . . . I do not suppose women can fully understand that fear. Not that particular one. We agonize instead over cancer, we take as a personal threat the lump in every friend's breast.

That was then. The Big C, we called cancer. Now we have the Big A, so front and center in our communal consciousness that I sometimes think it has displaced breast cancer and heart attacks — both hugely more treatable than twenty years ago

— as public enemy number one.

"We've had lawyers come in who are handling many cases at once," says the Columbia neuropsychologist Yaakov Stern. "They're worried. They'll say, 'I have to write everything down. I used to remember everything off the top of my head and I had sixty cases and had them all at my fingertips. Now I have to keep checking my notes.'

"I say to them, 'Yes, but as far as managing the cases and understanding the issues and so forth, do you feel like you're still doing that competently?'

" 'Well, yeah.'

"You know, a lot of us have complaints about our memories. I have complaints about mine." (At the time of our first interview, he was fifty.) "The key thing is, To what degree is it affecting your ability to do what you always do? Yes, a lot of us are forgetful because we have so much going on in our lives, and, yes, our memories do get worse as we get older, and, no, I don't feel my memory is as good as it was when I was twenty. But if someone were to ask me, Well, does it get in the way of your work? Can you still do what you want to do? Can you pay your bills? Can you do your job? Can you still run your life the way you're accustomed to running it?

"Yes. Of course I can. So that's the demarcation."

Those changes in the brain that affect our memories in such annoying ways begin to occur many, many years before we notice them. And they are distinctly different from the kinds of changes that occur with Alzheimer's disease. They are *different:* a crucial point to keep in mind. But many of us do not know that they are different. And many of us who know it do not keep it in mind.

We worry, for instance, when the brain's frontal lobes, which we need for retrieving episodic (autobiographical) memories, begin in midlife to do what frontal lobes do, which is to lose speed and volume. Being among the first areas of the brain to show change, they may stop giving us exactly what we want exactly when we want it. For instance, as I've noted, we may find ourselves hung up on memory for context: "I know I heard that story from *someone,* but I can't remember who," or "I just read about that, but I can't remember where."

These are the common, classic, tediously normal complaints, but we do not read them as normal. We read them as trouble. Signs and omens of the Big A.

Many specialists say that the kind of

normal memory loss we are talking about is not even a loss at all. It is a slowing — which is why the psychiatrist Margaret Sewell remarked (in Chapter Two), "You say you want to learn Italian when you're ninety? Okay! It is going to take you a little longer, but, assuming there's no pathology, you can do it!" She, and every other memory specialist I interviewed, made the same point: We expect and accept that our bodies will slow down with time. But not our minds.

"Your speed changes," Dr. Gordon says in his office in Baltimore. "You don't see boxers of fifty-five — they can't throw the punches fast enough. *Slowness is often confused with memory loss.*" (Italics mine.) "We see people in their forties and fifties who worry they're getting demented, when they're normal."

There is worry, and then there is *worry*. This kind is not the same as the unambivalent fear over the pain in the chest and the lump in the breast. This one is always undercut, or overlaid, by that funny little layer of pseudocomedy: It is both involved and distanced, scared and faintly amused, and deeply, deeply defensive. With that lump, with that chest pain, it is always evil agents — the genes, the fates — doing their dirty work upon us. They are traitorous inside jobs. They failed us. With memory, there is this awful sense that we are failing ourselves. So we get defensive and annoyed and turn the annoyance inward. Or outward.

That is when the self-defensive strategies kick in. Making jokes: "I can't even remember my own name anymore!" Finessing it: If the topic of conversation involves a forgotten name or fact or news event, changing the topic of conversation. Blaming others, a popular marital strategy, as in:

> "Why didn't you tell me I got that phone call?"
> "I did tell you."
> "No, you didn't."
> "Yes, I did. I told you last night. You just don't remember."
> "You did *not* tell me."

Of course, when the complaints get serious enough, many people stop talking about them. The self-defensive strategies of the Worried Well are frequently very different from the strategies people use when they really have something to worry about, as we will soon see.

Much has been made of "memory aids" — various nutritional supplements such as vitamins, herbs, and hormones. To my knowledge, no scientific study has shown that any of them provides any significant benefit for normal memory loss. (Though one supplement, as you'll find in Chapter Thirteen, on memory and diet, does seem to be slightly helpful to people who already have dementia.) But no matter. I know people who take stuff for memory and swear that it works, and here I side with the great sage Sinatra, who once said — or is said to have said — that he was in favor of anything that helps you get through the night. Provided, let's add with haste, that it does not hurt you or anyone else.

Which brings up smoking and drinking. Heavy users often claim that they cannot think well without their chosen poisons. But I know plenty of ex-heavy users for whom yesterday's chosen poison is today's pure poison, period. In a reaction precisely like my own, another ex-smoker tells me: "There was a time when I absolutely could not think without my cigarettes, and *knew* that I never would be able to. What can I tell you? Today, the very odor of cigarette smoke, the odor that used to clear my mind, clouds it up completely."

Some makers of those "memory boosters" advise using mnemonics, too — as boosters to the boosters, you might say. This tickles me to pieces, because it recalls a magazine article I once wrote about then-current diet crazes. In possibly the craziest of them all, you were given daily and very expensive injections of a substance called gonadotropic hormone. It was said to be a distillation of the urine of pregnant ewes, or some such thing, and guaranteed to make the pounds roll off.

Oh, and by the way — just incidentally, you understand — along with those injections, you also were put on a five-hundred-calorie-a-day diet. That's about three and a half lettuce leaves. *You bet* the pounds rolled off.

The Harvard psychologist Daniel L. Schacter says that some products touted as memory aids may have the same temporary "alerting" effect as a cup of coffee. More helpful (cheaper, too) are the simple mnemonic techniques that work the same way memory works: by association. Here are a few that have been useful to me and my pals. You may be using them already. If not, give them a try. None will stun you with the force of its inventiveness, but so what? They work.

Keep forgetting where you put the keys (the eyeglasses, the wallet, the etcetera)?

Would that all life's problems were so easy to solve: Consecrate a *place.* Put a hook in a wall right by the door, and that hook is the holy place for the keys. Fix the hook in plaster or wood; fix the association in cement.

So achingly obvious! Yet memory therapists say that misplacing the keys, or the whatever, remains one of the commonest complaints of the Worried Well. It is almost — dare I suggest? — as though we *wanted* to keep misplacing the keys, so that we could keep complaining about our terrible memories. A perverse tic of pride, like claiming the worst migraine in town or the longest surgical scar.

Keep forgetting to take your pills? Get in line.

This one involves prospective memory, which, as I have said, works two ways: time based (I must remember to take my pills at 7 a.m. and 7 p.m.) or event based (I must take my pills with food). Since time-based events are far harder to remember, the trick is to tie the two together. An example: I take a once-a-week calcium pill on Sundays. Sometimes I used to forget it. Now I keep the pill bottle on an end table right by the easy chair that I always settle into when I read the Sunday papers. No more forgetting.

Keep forgetting to turn off the oven or the stove?

After burning a couple of pots beyond redemption, I began keeping an alarm clock on my desk, where I work while things cook. (If your kitchen has all those swell digital bells and whistles, you are ahead of the game. I am not ahead of the game.) By now, burning those pots has carved itself so deep into my memory that it would probably not happen again. But I use the alarm clock anyway. Then I can relax, sort of, and concentrate on my work.

Forget whether you locked the door (closed the windows, turned off the lights, put out food for the dog)?

Try visual association, and use your other senses, too: *See* yourself going out the door, feel yourself pulling it shut, and fitting the key (it was hanging right there on its hook, right?) into the lock. Listen for the click of closure. The whole sensory exercise sharpens your powers of observation, and the more observant you are, the more you are likely to remember.

Forget why you went to the kitchen (bedroom, desk, colleague's office)?

If retracing your steps does not do the

trick, relax. Forget it, so to speak. That may help you remember it. What I assure you will *not* help is to stand there saying, "Damn, damn, damn, *what did I come in here for?*"

Memory cannot be forced: That's the point Cornell's Dr. Relkin makes (forcibly): "When you put a big effort into remembering something, you raise your anxiety level. And that sets off a series of events in the brain that are actually contrary to recollection. Which is why, in part, the memory comes back to you later, when you're not trying. When all that adrenaline is no longer circulating and the stakes are not as high, the mind relaxes, the associations flow more freely, and the word or name" (or the reason you went into the kitchen) "pops into your memory."

Do you have trouble memorizing telephone numbers?

Well, who doesn't, and anyway, you have them stored in your cell phone and in your computer and possibly even in some antediluvian way, like on paper.

But for the sheer joy of remembering — and also because remembering begets remembering — you might try this: Make words, however inane, out of letters corresponding to the numbers on the telephone keypad. My brother's number used to be 744-3926, which I couldn't ever remember until I transposed it into a memorable PIG EXAM (no reflection on my brother).

Or you can bunch together the digits. A friend, Norma Quine, who lives in a part of London where the first three digits are 422, uses the bunching technique: "My tennis club number is 5266. So I memorized it by saying, 5 plus 2 equals 7, and 6 plus 6 equals 12. And then all I need to remember is 7 and 12."

"But what would happen if you deconstructed that as 4 plus 3 and 7 plus 5?"

"That doesn't happen." The very act of doing that bunching exercise, it seems, helps to recall the correct digits.

As for everyone's favorite complaint — remembering names, the little devils — that one has a chapter all to itself, Chapter One, "Say Hello to Whatsisname."

Do you forget blocks of important information — the gist of a business meeting, a news report, a medical consultation?

Repetition, folks. Among memory experts, it is almost as holy a word as *association.* Keep repeating the high points; keep in mind that repeating them over time, coming back to them, say, several times a day, works far better than cramming.

And again, it always helps to elaborate on the memory by involving your other senses. Write out those high points. Each time you revisit them, say them aloud. Ask yourself questions about them.

Do you keep forgetting to make telephone calls, run errands, pay bills, show up for appointments?

I used to use one of those chic English leather appointment books, five by seven inches, with a week displayed on two facing pages and those miserly little blocks of space for each day. No! Pretend you're a dentist. Buy yourself one of those big fat uncompromisingly unstylish desk calendars that gives each day a full page of its own, and write down everything. Everything. Immediately, before you forget it. If you are not only forgetful but also as pathetically disorganized as I am, which you probably are not, this will really make a big difference in your life. I promise.

Do you forget what you were going to say or why you were going to say it? (Oh, my dear. *Constantly.*) If I had a sure solution I would bottle it. What I try to do — I think we all do it, instinctively — is retrace the conversational steps. Sometimes it works, and sometimes it goes more as it did in my living room last night:

"I can't remember what I started to say. What were we just talking about?"

"Well, you were saying how much you hate to fly . . ."

"No, before that."

"We were talking about vacations . . ."

"No, before that."

"I can't remember."

"But I was telling you a whole long story. Why did I start telling that story?"

"How should I know? It was your story."

And finally, the foolproof one: lists. First, and last, and always: lists. You can't put what you have forgotten to say on a list, but you can put most everything else. *Lists:* an aging frontal lobe's best friend.

It may be that we expect too much of our brains. We are more generous to our aching backs and our carpel-tunnel wrists, we respect their wear and tear. But do we appreciate how these frontal lobes have been performing through our lifetimes, dealing with the zillions of items of data that we have stuffed into them? Do we consider how the hippocampus, that miraculous memory center, not only looks like a seahorse (thus its name) but keeps working like a horse, a workhorse of traffic direction? Thankless work.

When they get it right, we take them for granted and when they get it wrong — meaning not fast enough, not *on demand* — we never stop to think, Well, now, these brain parts have been models of uncomplaining service, if not servitude, for so long, they deserve a little rest now and again. Not even a vacation — just the right, say, to move a little slower on the job, take an occasional coffee break, without our panicking.

Of course, some of the Worried Well will panic anyway.

"Maybe their memories are not as good as they used to be," Dr. Gordon says, "but the difference isn't much. They only *think* it is. They say, 'I'm so forgetful, I must be getting Alzheimer's.' But then you see them in a restaurant, checking out the bill. 'I've been charged $5.95 for this veal parmigiana, it should only be $5.50.'"

"That's a nineteen fifties menu," I say.

"That's veal parmigiana in Baltimore," he says, "not New York."

Chapter Twelve:
So When *Isn't* It
Normal?
OR, WHO HID MY KEYS?

Poor Alzheimer. It cannot be easy to rest in peace, knowing that the whole world curses your name.[*]

Alzheimer! I remember all too well — we all remember all too well what we most urgently want to forget — the first time I heard that name.

It was 1982. Heavy on my mind was the matter of my mother, a widow living alone outside Boston, with no complaints, ever, but she was frail and shy and her eyesight was bad and her hearing was worse and her English, she being foreign-born, was adequate but it wasn't the king's.

And this one night at 3 a.m. she wakes up, reaches for water, swallows denture-cleaning liquid instead, and panics. She thinks she has poisoned herself.

At dawn I get a call in New York from her

---

[*] Alois Alzheimer, 1864–1915, German neurologist who first diagnosed the disease.

doctor. He says, "She was so scared that I sent a police car to take her to the emergency room. A psychiatrist said she couldn't answer the simplest questions. He thinks it may be Alzheimer's and I have to tell you, I hope he's wrong, because we had that with my mother-in-law, and it's the worst thing you can imagine."

Thus heartened, I get up there fast and walk in prayerful dread into my mother's hospital room. There she sits, pink with embarrassment to see me, and at least as lucid as I.

"Well, you know me, I'm a scaredy-cat," she says, "and then, in the middle of the night I hear banging on the door, and two big policemen, like Cossacks," (Born to Russian Jews, she never forgot being hidden by her parents when Cossack troops raided their village.) "take me to a big bright room, and this doctor asks me a lot of funny questions.

"He asks, 'What is your telephone number?' I said, 'I don't remember.' Why should I remember? How often do I call myself?

"Then he says, 'Who won the war?' or 'Where was the war?' or something like that. I said, 'What war?' There have been *so many wars* — how did I know what war he meant?

"And then he asks me, 'Mrs. Weinman, where were you born?' So I said, 'I'm not sure.' So maybe he thought I was crazy. But, sweetheart, you *know* I'm not sure. One day they called it Russia, the next day they called it Poland, the next day it was Russia again."

I took her home, stayed a couple of days, then called from New York to ask how she was feeling.

"In the pinks!" she said. And so she was. No Alzheimer's.

I tell that story here because I know no clearer example, out of personal experience, of the impact of emotion — fear, rage, anything that gets the bad juices flowing — upon memory. Was it a memory problem? Not essentially. It was a 4 a.m. problem, a hearing problem, a language problem, a Cossack problem, and she thought she might die, and she was scared out of her mind. *Out of her mind.* It is often instructive when we stop to consider the literal meaning of a cliché.

And this, too: The examining doctor was young, inexperienced, probably exhausted, and just as supersensitive as all the rest of us to this looming specter of Alzheimer's disease. It was easy to make a knee-jerk diagnosis: *Doesn't know her own telephone number? Bingo! Alzheimer's!*

Which brings us to the issue of chic.

Alzheimer's disease is — please understand and write me no outraged letters, I do not use the word frivolously — Alzheimer's disease is chic.

Chic, of course, happens in medicine as everywhere else. Back in the sixties, in the era of Dr. Christiaan Barnard, the South African surgeon who did the world's first heart transplant, coronary surgery was chic.

In the seventies, in the heyday and aftermath of Masters and Johnson (no first names necessary; if that combination rings no bell, you are probably too young for this book), sex therapy was chic.

In the eighties and nineties it was AIDS, and AIDS, God knows, is still plenty with us, though no longer chic. Our instincts are generous but our attention spans are short.

Alzheimer's. A mere two decades ago, most of us knew little or nothing about it, and many of us had never even heard the name. How did it get from there to here?

Partly by the massive, well-financed efforts of the Alzheimer's Foundation of America and other such organizations. Partly it was the sad, graceful saga of Ronald and Nancy Reagan that reached via television into all our lives. Partly it was, and is, the old follow-the-money story: Government has huge interest in supporting Alzheimer's research because Alzheimer's costs government a fortune. Patients go to nursing homes, family resources run out, Medicaid kicks in. As for American businesses, between insurance costs and the absenteeism of primary caregivers, the annual tab exceeds $60 billion. Overall, the disease costs the nation close to $150 billion a year.

But mainly, this is the story of a generation: the seventy-eight million baby boomers born between 1946 and 1964.

Three and a half million of them, including Bill Clinton and George W. Bush, were born in that first year. They were in diapers when television was also in diapers, in their teens when John F. Kennedy was elected, in their twenties when Woodstock exploded in tribal ecstasy, in their thirties when John Lennon was murdered, in their forties when Ronald Reagan announced that he had Alzheimer's disease, and in their fifties when the new millennium rolled in, by which time many of them were complaining more about remembering less.

Now those first baby boomers are in their sixties, and the younger ones keep coming along to join in the chorus of complaints.

In recent years, major news-magazine cover stories have reported that Alzheimer's disease is now *the* biggest health concern of the boomer generation. Is it just the usual hyperbole of news-magazine cover stories? Hard to say, because the evidence is mainly anecdotal. But here is what I was told by Dr. Richard E. Powers, who is chairman of the scientific advisory committee of the Alzheimer's Foundation and may know as much about the disease as anyone in the country:

"I believe it absolutely. Look at the psychological profile of the boomers — and I am one — with their stress on youth. This is the generation that wanted to be young forever, and now they're finding that it's not going to happen. Alzheimer's is the most feared disease of our generation because it is linked to autonomy and independence and because — I can tell you this, having given talks to thousands of well boomers — because what is *major* for them is holding onto their intellects."

Dr. Powers is fifty-six. Does he have memory problems?

Laughter, subdued. "I was recently with a group of doctors, all about my age, and we were all laughing about the changes we all observe. When we were twenty-five and thirty-five we could read a scientific article once and hold on to the whole thing. Now we have to read it several times.

"A few years ago I started losing names. It doesn't mean I have dementia; it means that I am fifty-six and my ability to hold on to new information is not as good as it used to be. You know, that flypaper in the brain — it's like flypaper that's been lying a long time on the counter. It's still got plenty of stick to it, but not as much as it used to have."

The It Must Be Alzheimer's Syndrome even affects the *babies* of baby boomers. As I write this, I am recalling a recent conversation with my dental hygienist, she doing most of the talking because my mouth was otherwise occupied:

I: How's your memory? (A question I put, these days, to practically everyone I meet.)

EVELYN: Terrible. It's always been terrible. I've heard that people who have always had a bad memory are more likely to get Alzheimer's disease. Is that true?

I: No.

EVELYN: No? Really? Well, that's good to know. But I do worry about it. I mean, I'm not *constantly* worrying. But sometimes I feel sure that I'll be getting it, because my memory is so bad. Yeah (*industriously scraping away at a nugget of plaque in my mouth*), I really do worry about it.

Evelyn is thirty-eight.

The primary risk factor for Alzheimer's disease is age. Not intelligence, not lifestyle, not genetics — though, as we will soon see, they all seem to play a role — but age.

"Relatively few people used to make it to fifty," says Barry Gordon, the Johns Hopkins neurologist. "Now, with so many infectious diseases conquered, with heart disease so much more treatable — and with the high-performance demands of our culture — the big fear for many people is not that they're going to keel over from a heart attack. It's Alzheimer's."

Columbia University's Dr. Yaakov Stern, who also is director of neuropsychology at the Memory Disorders Center of the New York State Psychiatric Institute, adds: "We used to see less Alzheimer's because people died before they were really at risk. Now we live in a world where more and more people are living longer. So all of a sudden, over the last twenty years, let's say, the problem has really exploded."

I ask, "Are you suggesting that if we all lived long enough, we would all wind up with Alzheimer's?"

"No! What I'm saying is simply that the percentage of people who have it gets higher with advancing age."

"So if you scientists are going to keep finding ways to make us live longer, you'd better also come up with ways to cure the disease."

"Yes," says Dr. Stern. "That's the issue."

And so for us, the Worried Well, the big question arises: When is it normal, age-appropriate memory loss, and when is it (possibly) something more?

Symptomatically, the two may seem, at first, not to be so different — which is what gets normal people crazy with worry. But physiologically, they are dramatically different.

Normal memory loss happens because brains start to shrink, blood flow starts to ebb, and chemical neurotransmitters start to do less of whatever it is that they do . . . and why the surprise? We tend not to want to believe that the brain bone is connected to the knee bone, but these things happen as naturally as eyes' weakening and bones' brittling and upper arms' starting to go flabby. If you luck into longevity, they come with the territory, for almost everyone. (Except for the flabby arms, which seem, damn it, to have a certain specificity of gender. My gender.)

Alzheimer's disease happens because of a distinct pattern of abnormal changes that occur in the brain. Neurons become entangled so that they can no longer fire. Deposits of a protein called amyloid build up and form plaque. This amyloid stuff blocks traffic, just as a different kind of plaque may block traffic in the coronary arteries. It gums up the works, and it leads ultimately to the death of brain tissue.

More is *not* known about Alzheimer's than is known.

It is not known, for example, how to diagnose it by dependable clinical means, such as a brain scan or a blood test.

It is not known who will be stricken.

It is not known why fully two-thirds of its victims are women (surprised? I was flabbergasted), although an at-least-partial answer lies in the simple fact that women live longer. Also, women have a harder time controlling diabetes, obesity, and high cholesterol, all risk factors for Alzheimer's.

And, as most of us seem to be aware, there

is currently no known cure. There are horizons of hope, which we will get to. And because, despite recent progress, there is still no fully reliable medical test, there is no absolute certainty of a correct diagnosis. (Posthumously, yes, by autopsy. Cold comfort.)

But there are rules of thumb, Dr. Stern says.

"We give a battery of tests — memory tests, language tests, puzzles, spatial and reasoning ability. We look for a pattern of deficits typical of early Alzheimer's, and we make the call. We're most often right. The question is, with subtler problems, how to make that call. We use norms that show the expected performance at a given age, adjusted for gender, education, and so on. Someone may have a decline that will not show as a bad score, based on the norms, because he started from a higher baseline of abilities twenty years ago — but we didn't know him twenty years ago. That's what makes our role difficult in making the differential diagnosis."

If someone scores significantly lower than the norm *and* has memory complaints (or others have complaints about him) but can still function well in daily life, the diagnosis is *mild cognitive impairment.* It may remain mild or it may progress into Alzheimer's or even improve. It's the classic "Only time will tell."

For the Worried Well, there are rules of thumb, too. In this, as in so much else, it is mainly a matter of degree. For instance: You come home from a busy day at the office and somebody says, "Did you remember to get the milk?" You slap your head or snap your fingers, whatever your style of rue may be, and say, "Tch! I forgot." Not to worry.

On the other hand, if you say, "What milk?" and if this happens with increasing frequency, it may be another story.

IS IT NORMAL?

Probably Normal	**Possibly Worri-some**
• You often misplace things.	• You constantly misplace things and may blame other people.
• You forget what the social plans are and ask, "What did you say we are doing tonight?"	• A half hour later, you ask again.

216

- Occasionally you forget where you parked the car.

- You tell the world that your memory is terrible.

- You sometimes forget to keep appointments, run errands, make calls, take pills.
- Sometimes you forget what you ate last night.
- You know you have some memory loss but can run your life the way you want to.
- You forget the names of new acquaintances.

- You often forget where you parked and sometimes forget a familiar route.

- Others complain about your memory. You tend to worry silently.

- These are increasingly common lapses.

- Much of yesterday is often a blank.
- Your memory loss interferes with daily functioning.

- You forget the names of close friends and relatives.

- People sometimes say, "You already told me that."

- It is much harder for you than it used to be to handle several tasks at once.

- You are frequently and unknowingly repeating yoursclf.

- You simply cannot do it.

"It may be a judgment that's hard for the person himself to make," Dr. Stern says. "Someone else will say, 'He thinks he's doing okay, but he's making mistakes. He's really not handling things well . . .' That's a telling issue. But I think that, on the rule-of-thumb level, what's most important is if you yourself find that you just can't do things that came easily to you before. A lot of us walk around with 'Oh, my memory isn't as good as it used to be . . .' But usually, what brings people to the doctor's office is when something happens."

"Such as?"

"Someone makes a big mistake at work. Kids visit their parents and see that bills aren't being paid. The house looks messy. The mother used to cook these beautiful meals and she never does anymore — not because she's uninterested but because she just can't manage it. The bridge partners are complaining. Now that's a very good example, because bridge is a high-cognition skill. You hear, 'My partners won't play with me anymore. They say I'm making too many mistakes.' "

Metacognition: that is our own perception of our own abilities. If you have complaints about your memory and you test (*if* you test; given the lack of a cure, you might choose not to) normal, the problem may be one of these:

1. You have a fuller plate of tasks than you used to have.
2. You started out, when you were younger, with more cognitive capacity than the norm; time has been catching up with you.
3. You are simply unaccustomed to garden-variety memory loss.

Your memory may be just fine. It is not as good at fifty as it was at thirty, but it seems plenty good enough to the people around you. But that is not *your* perception.

"You know," says the New York neurologist Gayatri Devi, "there is a big difference between a brain that is functioning at a hundred percent and a brain that is functioning at ninety-five percent. A huge difference. Far greater than the difference between a brain that's functioning at fifty percent, say, and one that's functioning at thirty percent, *in terms of a person's self-perception.*" (Italics mine.)

I've suggested earlier that most of us are perverse enough to enjoy kvetching about our forgetfulness. As long as we do so — "You think *you* have memory problems? Let me tell you . . ." — it is probably nothing to worry about. But when people sense that they have a real problem, Dr. Devi says, many tend to stop talking about it, certainly stop joking about it, and instead start trying to hide it, even from close family members.

Previously voluble people may withdraw, which can make them appear depressed — and, of course, they may well be depressed, with the memory they used to rely upon failing them now. But it may also be that they stop talking simply because they are afraid of using the wrong word or saying something stupid. Or they may develop what she calls a cocktail personality.

"They'll have a conversation with you that consists completely of chitchat, with no pieces of information, so that you don't realize that they have a problem. They learn to talk for hours without having to give any information."

Then there is the blame game, a major strategy to cover one's tracks. It was Dr. Devi who described the classic cohabitational exchange: "I *told* you we were going out this evening."

"No, you didn't!"

"Yes I did!"

"No you didn't!"

But when there is serious worry, the blame game is no strategy. It may morph from "I can't remember where I left my keys" into "Who moved my keys?" and then, possibly, into *"Why did you take my keys?"*

Which pretty much encapsulates the distinctions among normal memory loss, mild cognitive impairment, and dementia.

Among the hottest topics in memory research now is how to make early detection of Alzheimer's.

"Early, *early* detection. Can we pick up a problem before it gets bad? That's the goal researchers set for themselves now," Dr. Stern says.

"Why now more than they used to?"

"Because the medications we have don't do anything for the pathology. They just keep a person from declining as fast. But now there's the possibility that soon there may be medications that get at the root cause of the disease, so that you could block this pathology in its early stages, before it's had a chance to do a lot of damage. Mild cognitive impairment: that's the issue that's being pushed by drug houses now, on the theory that earlier intervention may stave off progression."

I confess to a poisonous suspicion that another theory of the drug houses may be that earlier intervention may mean more sales; but then, I tend to a poisonous view of the drug houses.

A second hot topic is the study of old people whose memories are intact. The ones who sail through their eighties and nineties with barely so much as a Whatsisname. I hardly need note that their numbers, may their tribe increase, are small.

Why do they stay so well ahead of the game? Well, *because.* Because, despite our fine democratic rhetoric, no two brains are created equal. Like natural athletes, some people may be born with a neurological leg up, with more intrinsic skills for remembering. Some people may have genes that provide an extra margin of protection against dementia.

But also, it seems increasingly apparent,

environmental differences play a big, big role.

Dr. Stern speaks of "brain reserve" — some people have larger brains, more neurons — and of his own concept of "cognitive reserve." Think of it as a kind of mental hedge fund. Genes, IQ, and life experiences — level of education, type of occupation, diet, leisure activities, social networks, mental and physical exercise — all seem to enrich the hedge fund.

"When brain damage occurs, the brain doesn't just sit still and take it," he says. "It tries to compensate for the damage; it does its best to cope. We see two people with the same amount of brain damage, yet one seems demented and the other seems normal. That's the one with more cognitive reserve. The more cognitive reserve there is, the better the brain can cope."

Using brain scans, his research team has found that some people will use different neural pathways than others to solve the same problem, and will solve it more efficiently. It seems that those life experiences that contribute to cognitive reserve may actually alter the way the brain works, enabling it to function with greater efficiency and flexibility. Now they are designing a study to learn more about how cognitive reserve works and how it can be enhanced. *That's* what I call a no-risk hedge fund.

At Mount Sinai Hospital in New York, Professor Jeremy Silverman heads a team that is studying people over age ninety, "the oldest of the old," who pretty much have all their marbles — the cognitively intact, as they say in the trade. They are looking at these rare birds from both genetic and environmental points of view.

Four different genes are identified with Alzheimer's. Three are rare and can lead to the disease at very young ages, even in the thirties, and we needn't concern ourselves with them here. The fourth one is called apolipoprotein E. It is common, and it comes in three flavors, just as genes for eye color, as Dr. Silverman helpfully points out, come in various flavors such as brown, blue, and hazel.

These three flavors are designated E2, E3, and E4. E2 is the rarest, as bad luck would have it, because there is some evidence that it protects against Alzheimer's. It occurs in about eight percent of the general population. E4, the gene associated with higher risk, is found in about eighteen percent. Genes, of course, come in pairs, one from each parent. People who carry a pair of

E3's, or an E3 and an E4, would be at less risk than those with a pair of E4's.

The Silverman team is studying a particular population in Costa Rica, a group of families with a number of cognitively intact family members over age ninety. Only two percent of these elders seem to carry the higher-risk gene. Their relatives are more likely to have reduced risk, too, Dr. Silverman says.

But none of this is to suggest that genes have the weight in Alzheimer's that they have in, say, Huntington's disease, which is strongly hereditary.

If you carry a pair of E4 genes but are in good health, you do not necessarily end up with Alzheimer's. On the other hand, the E2's may not help you much if you also have hypertension or high cholesterol or diabetes or obesity — all risk factors — and do not follow doctors' orders.

(In fact, shocking numbers of Americans do not follow doctors' orders. "We're a noncompliant nation," says the Alzheimer Foundation's Dr. Richard Powers. "About forty-six percent of diabetics take medications as they should. In hypertension, forty percent take them right, twenty percent take them sometimes, and forty percent simply don't take them.")

To neglect a disorder such as midline (belly) obesity, which would seem to have nothing whatever to do with cognition, is really to ask for trouble. "People think of obesity as a kind of suitcase sticking out in front of you," Dr. Powers says. "But that fat is also on the inside, it is stuck to your organs, and it is changing your body's chemistry in ways that may be harmful to your brain cells."

Seeing as how we are stuck with our genes, you may well wonder, as I did, what use it is to explore the genetic makeup of a bunch of wondrously intact nonagenarians. Ah, but, says Dr. Silverman, "The more we can learn about which genes confer protection against dementia, the greater the likelihood that it will lead to interventions — pills or diets or something else — that may do for people what the good genes do."

Gazing into the future, some specialists are less inclined to see a cure for Alzheimer's disease than increasingly effective medications that would control it and slow it down. But many others see a genuine silver bullet — something that would go directly to the root cause of the disease.

On the near horizon are various approaches that might provide the bullet. Scientists are targeting amyloid, the protein that builds up into plaques and leads to Alzheimer's. Genes may give someone a tendency to develop the plaques, and the scientists are experimenting with drugs to block that action. They are exploring ways to develop the immune system to fight against the amyloid. They are developing antibodies that stick to the amyloid and may help clear it out of the brain.

"There's an assumption that eventually we will have a treatment," Dr. Stern says. "I think that maybe, within five years, there will be active clinical trials."

It would be a sea change. What we have now is, in a way, what we had with cancer a quarter-century ago, before the advent of early interventions and dramatically effective treatments. Many of us can remember a time when cancer was so frightening that nobody talked about it and, if there was any in the family, it was kept quiet, like something shameful. A silver bullet for Alzheimer's disease would cancel out that great boomer burden of fear and anxiety overnight. Because, after all, what makes the disease so frightening is not so much the disease itself as the lack of a cure.

Finally we come to the environmental side of the street. Professor Michal Beeri works that side for the Mount Sinai studies.

Discussing the reasons that Alzheimer's strikes mostly women, including their susceptibility to such high-risk diseases as diabetes and hypertension, she raised the estrogen issue:

Women stop producing estrogen after menopause — men continue to produce it, in testosterone, though in diminishing amounts as they age — and low estrogen levels are thought to be another risk factor for Alzheimer's. (But, whoa. There is no good evidence that hormone-replacement therapy would offer protection.)

Now Dr. Beeri brought up yet another theory, which is related to childbirth:

The more children a woman has, the lower her estrogen level. And so it may be that a woman with multiple childbirths is at somewhat greater risk. Which does *not* mean that women with lots of children need be fearful, or that women who want lots of children shouldn't have them. It means only that one of the many risk factors in this enormously complex picture may be multiple births — and perhaps not even because of low estrogen levels but for some wholly other reason, such as the possibility that having more children may provoke more stress, and stress is a known risk factor. As I said earlier, more is not known than is known.

None of which, at any rate, ranks near the three top risk factors, which are these:

1. Age
2. Gender
3. Education

As to age: Okay, it's a trade-off. Die younger, have less chance of getting the disease. I'll happily take my chances.

As to gender: Well, there is nothing to be done about gender. But women can do plenty about controlling those factors, such as obesity, cholesterol, diabetes, that put them at higher risk than men.

As to education: Dr. Stern recalls being contacted by an editor of *Seventeen* magazine, who was interested in publishing an article about cognitive reserve. "Well, I was puzzled. All I knew about *Seventeen* magazine was that my fourteen-year-old daughter had outgrown it. So I said, 'Why are you interested in cognitive reserve?' and this editor said, 'For the message: *Stay in school!*' "

Many studies have linked education to Alzheimer's, but Dr. Stern has a statistic that startled me: "In our study, people with fewer than eight years' education were at *twice* the risk for Alzheimer's disease."

But, of course, it is not simply education. It is a package deal. People with less education are apt to be less economically secure, to work in less challenging jobs, to get less mental stimulation, get less physical exercise, have less leisure activity, have fewer social and cultural pursuits, follow less healthy diets — in short, to have less of all those generally middle-class perks that feed into cognitive reserve.

Dr. Beeri says, "When I give lectures, I tell people, 'Watch your cholesterol. Control your weight. Be strict in taking your medications. Be mentally active. Be physically active. Be socially active.' Now, none of these is terribly difficult to do. But put them all together, and you very likely decrease the risk of developing Alzheimer's disease.

"I always stress the social factor. The importance of reading, say, doesn't seem so complicated. It's sort of like activating a muscle. But when we talk about maintaining a social network, that's much more complex.

"Why should having a close social network protect against dementia? Because love is good for the brain? Because if you have people who talk to you every day, you are not so lonely, and that is good for the brain?

Because if you stay in touch with others, they are sensitive to your health and send you to a doctor when they see trouble?

"We don't know. But when I lecture, I say, 'Listen, guys, make friends! Keep your social life alive! Because it does good things for you!' "

Yo, friend.

P.S. Oh, and about my mother: She lived five more years after that tentative diagnosis of Alzheimer's, to the age of eighty-six. And if I'm still around at eighty-six, with a memory as keen as hers . . . well, let me wish it upon us all.

CHAPTER THIRTEEN: YOU SAY BRAIN FOOD, I SAY SPINACH

DIET AND MEMORY

"You know," she said, "my memory is much better since I discovered this magic potion."

"What magic potion?" I asked.

"Ginkgo biloba."

"You're kidding."

"What do you mean, I'm kidding?"

"Well, it's been pretty much disproved —"

"Disproved by *whom?*"

"Most of the research has shown —"

"I don't care about *research.* I am talking about *my personal experience.*"

At which point any fool would have known to back off. Which I didn't do.

"I'm only saying that there's no hard evidence —"

"That's what *you* say," she said.

And that was it. We finished lunch and we said a sodden good-bye and she has been put out with me ever since, and I don't really blame her. You do not rain on some-body else's parade. You do not knock some-body else's magic potion. It is like knocking somebody else's doctor or mother or, God forbid, religion. Sacred ground. Keep Off the Grass. Don't even *think* of parking there.

When it comes to faith in a cure-all, research does not matter. Faith matters. It is like those immortal words spoken long ago by a member of the Revlon cosmetic dynasty: "What we sell," he said, "is hope." They sell it, we buy it.

Take even the most cursory romp through self-help sites on the Web and you will find arm-long scrolls of edible substances, each one of which somebody swears is the world's best memory booster.

A brief list: horse chestnut seed extract (which you would perhaps recognize more readily by its Latin name, *Aesculus hippocastanum*), echinacea, saw palmetto, ginkgo, boron, black cohosh, St. John's wort, milk thistle, horny goat weed, ginseng, evening primrose, valerian . . . and moving along into less-exotic-sounding territory, we come to alfalfa, beans (kidney, lima, soy), flaxseed oil, green tea, grape juice, choco-late, chewing gum, fenugreek, lavender, pomegranate juice, cranberries, ginger, artichoke, carrot, cabbage, pumpkin, garlic and garlic powder, omega-3 fatty acids, hydrochloric acid, iron, kelp, licorice extract, nickel, pine bark extract, red clover, seeds (sunflower, sesame, flax, pumpkin), a slew of vitamins (most popularly, C, E, and an assortment of B's), a raft of minerals, innumerable herbal brews . . . on and on and on. Send no indignant letters about the omissions. Space prevents, etc. Besides, if there is an end to the list, I couldn't find it.

It may be that every one of these items helps memory. Many contain antioxidants, which are said to help protect brain cells against damage, and so people may reasonably assume that they help memory, too. Nobody can prove that they don't. But so far, nobody has proven that they do.

So here is the question: What can we put into our mouths that is known to help our memories?

Here is the answer: "Basically, there are no solidly proven dietary factors for the preservation of memory."

Ouch.

The question was mine. The answer came from Dr. Meir Stampfer, professor of epidemiology and nutrition at the Harvard School of Public Health.

He then added a big *But:* "But what is most promising is the evidence showing a link between vascular disease and dementia. Diets associated with a lower risk of vascular disease are also associated with a lower risk of dementia. If you eat a heart-healthy diet, you are also eating a brain-healthy diet."

They all say it. They say it in uncannily the same way. I put the same question to Dr. William Jagust, professor of public health and neuroscience at the University of California, Berkeley. Answer: "The overwhelming evidence is that a diet that is heart-healthy is also brain-healthy. It's not clear why all this is. The simple explanation is that the brain is supplied by blood vessels and whatever you do for your blood vessels will ultimately benefit your brain. I doubt it's that simple. But whatever the reasons, the data are just overwhelming."

What, then, about dietary supplements? Aha. A whole other kettle of fish oil.

Dr. Stampfer is the medical editor of a major report on dietary supplements published by the Harvard Medical School. There were two reports: one — his — on vitamins and minerals, and the other on herbal and other preparations.

Dietary supplements are an eighteen-billion-dollar-a-year industry. Millions of people use them for treatment of everything from high blood pressure to ulcerative colitis to obsessive-compulsive disorder to male-pattern hair loss to the only subject that concerns us here, our memories.

These supplements are not government regulated, as prescription medications are. Until last summer, when the Food and Drug Administration finally bestirred itself to set new standards for accurate labeling and quality control, the manufacturers never had to list all their ingredients, indicate quantities of ingredients, or submit to quality control. We have had a self-policing system, and, judging by the Harvard Medical School reports, much of the police force has been out to lunch. Manufacturers can never claim that supplements treat or cure diseases. But there is nothing to stop them from making come-on label claims such as "boosts sexual desire," "strengthens immune system," "relieves stress," or, more to our point, "improves memory."

The authors of the Harvard reports use the good-news-bad-news formula. The good news, they write, is that because more research is being done, we are learning more about these substances. The bad news is what we are learning: "The bad news is that with increasing scientific scrutiny, problems with herbs and other supplements are coming to light."

Most problems are with herbs, not vitamins. About vitamins, they say essentially: There is no scientific evidence (despite longtime buzz) that vitamin E helps the memory of healthy people; an E-rich diet (whole grains, vegetable oils, and the usual leafy green vegetables) may help protect against Alzheimer's, but it is unclear if E supplements would do the same; antioxidants are good and our bodies produce them, but the value of antioxidant supplements is uncertain. People with low levels of folic acid and B_6 and B_{12} seem to do less well in memory tests, so a multivitamin is good for almost everyone. Overdosing (of *anything*) is bad and could be dangerous. For example, too much E could cause bleeding in anyone who takes blood thinners, such as Coumadin.

As for herbal supplements, problem one: Many of the products considered in the Harvard report do not contain what they claim to contain. Problem two: Some contain so little of the active ingredient that it is not significantly measurable. Problem three: Many do not effectively treat the conditions they claim to treat.

The researchers tested fifty-two herbal supplements, of which the ten top sellers in the country are garlic, echinacea, saw palmetto, ginkgo biloba, cranberry, soy, ginseng, black cohosh, St. John's wort, and milk thistle. Although they are all touted on Web sites as memory boosters, only ginkgo is marketed as such. So let us, for the moment, stick with that one.

Ginkgo has long been the prom queen of the memory industry. In recent years several studies fizzled, and in some quarters the prom queen became a wallflower. Sales dropped way down, though they are still huge; hope has legs. (In fact, despite the popularity of herbal products, total sales have been dropping in this country for the past decade. Whenever a supplement gets good spin from a clinical test, there is a sharp upward spike on the downward trajectory, but still it has been a downward trajectory. Why? Depends on whom you ask. Either it's because people tried them, found no lasting benefit, and stopped buying them or because people tried them and found such lasting benefit that they no longer needed them. Pay your money, take your pick.)

In analyzing various ginkgo products for quality and purity, the researchers found big differences in the amount of active ingredient from one to the next. They also found that many of those products were not manufactured according to recommended standards. The new FDA rules on labeling and manufacturing standards will not apply to all makers until 2010, and they *still* do not require supplements to be proven effective before they are sold.

So how do you know what you're getting? Well, you don't. Unless you do some homework and go, as the Harvard reports very helpfully suggest that we do, to such reputable medical Web sites as www.clinicaltrials.gov, to learn which products have been tested, and how they scored.

To grade effectiveness, the researchers use an herbal report card.

A means that there is "strong scientific evidence" for the use of a certain substance for a certain condition.

B means that there is "good scientific evidence" for its use.

C means that there is "no clear scientific evidence" for its use.

And on downward. D means . . . *Forget* it (at least according to current research), and, if I were you and suspected that I was getting a D benefit out of some A-touted product, I would hightail it to my local bookstore or library or friendly resident Google to check out the Harvard reports.

For the treatment of Alzheimer's disease and vascular dementia, ginkgo scored an A. (Several studies have shown that it may temporarily help Alzheimer's patients, or at least slow thc progression of the disease.) But for *us* — to improve garden-variety, age-related memory loss — and as a "memory booster" for healthy people of all ages, it scored a C.

In fact, almost everything scored a C. I have never seen so many C's gathered in one place. I rough-counted them: Out of 280-plus grades given to 52 supplements, there were 14 A's, some 30 B's, 26 D's (ginkgo scored only one D, as a preventive treatment for stroke), and the rest were all C's.

Which does not *necessarily* mean that those products have no value. Tests proceed apace. The most seemingly reliable research today may be canceled out by newer research tomorrow. That is part of the scientific process. It is also part of the problem.

"There have been a lot of terrible studies, highly over-interpreted," Dr. Stampfer says. "And of course there is a lot of vested interest. For a substance to be absolutely proven through randomized trials, where you put some people on the substance and others on a placebo and you follow them over a period of time and find a significant difference — therc are no such studies."

What there are plenty of, are variables. The designs of tests vary. Dosages vary. Populations vary. One study shows negative results, meaning that substance X did not live up to its claims. Another shows positive results, meaning that it did. Unbeknownst to us, a positive study may have some connection to the manufacturer of a substance X product, while a negative study has been independently sponsored. In short — and every authority I have interviewed makes the same point, often in the same phrase — the jury is still out.

So we are left to our own devices. Which is not such a bad place to be, really. It would be a terrible place to be if we were dealing with treatments for life-threatening diseases. But this is not a burning question (except, of course, for the captains of the dietary-supplement industry). We are not talking about some unsubstantiated "cure" for cancer; we are talking about whether or not dietary supplements can goose our balky memories. The jury of experts may still be out, but we have the expertise of our own experience.

Which brings me back to my (possibly former) friend, the ginkgo devotee. Her experience tells her that ginkgo is gold. My experience may tell me that ginkgo is spinach. But if I could replay that lunch date, I would not lecture her about the research. I would say, "If it works for you, it works." And let it go at that.

Why? First, *because* the jury is still out. Her faith may yet turn out to be scientifically well founded.

Second: If it is pure placebo effect, so what? Placebo effects can be terrific. They have brought an awful lot of comfort to an awful lot of people.

Third, and always a consideration: Say that in a test of substance X, ninety-eight percent of the respondents report that it did nothing for them. Only two percent report that it helped. But if you are in that two percent, substance X was *one hundred percent* effective — *for you.*

I confess that sometimes, as I zap through endless TV commercials and contemplate those urgent pharmacological entreaties to try various products for "sexual desire disorder" — too much desire? too little? what are they talking about? — and "social anxiety syndrome" and so forth . . . sometimes it does seem to me that, in the fullness of their creativity, our drug houses do not so much invent pills to treat conditions as they invent conditions to sell pills.

They medicalize normality. They market potions to treat disorders that never used to be considered disorders, such as the slight benign sluggishness of our memories, which most neuroscientists agree is a normal part of our aging, and brilliantly they convince us that it is not normal, that it is a condition about which something can and must be done, and so we buy those potions to the tune of billions of dollars a year, although there is remarkably little scientific evidence that they have any effect at all.

Well, that's how I feel on the one hand. On the other, if they came up with some booster for memory that looked really promising, would I buy it?

Friends, I'd be first in line.

Now we come to the proven stuff. We come to the diet called *caloric restriction.* It will not get your gastric juices flowing, but it could be the first step toward what everyone has been seeking since the start of recorded time: a way to slow the aging process. Which includes, up front and center, the aging of memory.

It began with the monkeys. If you had seen them, staring out from newspaper pages in late 2006, you would not be likely to soon forget them: a pair of the saddest-looking simians anyone ever saw.

They were participants, however unwillingly, in a study at the Wisconsin National Primate Research Center, and they had plenty to be sad about. Both were twenty-eight years old, which, for a monkey, is no spring chicken. But only one looked old. That was the one on a normal, fairly high-calorie diet. The other one looked healthy and vital and youthful but equally miserable; and if you were fed what he was being fed, you would be miserable, too.

There was also a picture of a man. The man was smiling, although he didn't look too well, either. There was a caption saying that the man was six feet tall and weighed 135 pounds. There was a picture of the man's lunch, which showed why a person would be six feet tall and weigh 135 pounds: fermented soybeans and a few leaves of green, yum-yum. It really was a pathetic-looking plate of food.

Despite that wan grin, the man said that he felt just fine. He said, "Mostly I do the diet to be healthier, but if it helps me live longer, hey, I'll take that, too."

There came floating into my consciousness the ancient gag: Cut out fats, booze, and sex and you can live to be 120. If you don't die of boredom first.

He was talking about caloric restriction, known to aficionados, of whom there are not many, as CR, known to me as the Diet from Hell.

Scientists have long known that a severely restricted diet, nutritious but thirty to forty percent reduced in calories, can produce dramatic results in various animals, including monkeys and mice. The diet somehow alters the molecular processes that cause aging. It slows everything down. (Think turtles, who can survive without food for months at a time, slow their metabolism down to a crawl, and live — at a crawl — for two hundred years.)

For decades, the scientists knew that it happened without understanding *how* it happened. But the enormous discovery they have made in recent years is that the aging process can be regulated. It is controlled by certain genes, and caloric restriction activates these genes.

What happens is a biological kind of knee-bone-thigh-bone chain reaction: CR switches on a gene that produces a good enzyme that protects the cells against a bad enzyme that contributes to aging.

It may be a built-in survival mechanism: When you are taking in so little nourishment, the body feels under stress, just as it would in a time of famine. So it conserves energy by slowing everything down, by switching on its "longevity" genes. It is doing what bodies must have done through those tens of thousand of years in which our ancestors went forth to hunt and to gather and sometimes, perhaps for years at a time, found the pickings mighty slim. So their biology went on the defensive.

Moral of the story: *We were never meant to eat so much.*

We may cultivate it and cook it and eat it and overeat it and find it finger-lickin' good, but our biology is still back there with those ancestral hunters and gatherers. We were not designed for the incursions of a Big Mac and fries.

So those monkeys may not be happy campers but they live longer than their fatter brethren and they are more resistant to age-related diseases such as diabetes and cardiac and neurodegenerative diseases — which include cognitive impairment.

Many researchers believe that the diet can work for people, too. Well, then. Since it can extend the life span, and since it can protect against abnormal consequences of aging, might it also protect against *normal* consequences of aging? You can see where we're going here: The implications for normal memory loss are terrific.

The trouble is, who can stay on such a diet? The six-foot, 135-pound man is one of several thousand stout (skinny) souls in the country who swear by CR. There is even a Caloric Restriction Society. But for most of us, the diet is simply too severe to sustain.

Which brings us from the monkeys to the mice.

Soon after that news story about the monkeys came reports about experiments being done with mice at Harvard Medical School and at the National Institute on Aging.

The researchers had divided their mice into two groups. Group A ate a high-calorie diet and plumped up in the predictable way and developed all the predictable symptoms — physical frailty, incipient diabetes, cardiac disease, the mouse equivalent of Alzheimer's, the works. Group B was kept on exactly the same diet and plumped up equally — but did not develop any of those symptoms. There they were, scarfing down the fats and carbs yet staying vigorous and alert, and living longer. If ever there was a perfect example of having one's cake and eating it too, these mice were it.

The difference was that the Group B mice

were also given massive amounts of a chemical called resveratrol. As you may have read at the time, this is the stuff — a molecule, actually — that is found in red wine, and it is one of a class of substances that may yet turn out to be the holy grail of anti-aging. Researchers disagree about how it works, but it seems to mimic the good effects of CR. Or, to put it the other way around: It seems to offset the bad effects of your average all-American diet.

Resveratrol may explain that long-recognized phenomenon called the French paradox: Traditionally, the French have eaten richer food — all those lovely, lethal cream-and-butter sauces — than we Americans but had less heart disease. Why?

One theory attributes it to their generous consumption of red wine. This theory has been taken as gospel for many decades, although it may not be true, which has never stopped anything from being taken as gospel.

It could be, for example, that the French had less heart disease because they consumed fewer calories, despite those traditional rich sauces. (But *do* they still consume fewer calories? There are now some 1,100 McDonald's restaurants in France, and the few I have seen were always Standing Room

Only — although, as you may recall, one Frenchman, in a rush of Gallic pride and fury, once plowed his truck right through one of their storefronts.) Or it may be that the French walk more than we do, neutralizing the harm they do with their mouths by the good they do with their legs.

Whatever the explanation, anyone who wanted to give resveratrol a try — and swarms of people did — could readily buy any number of over-the-counter dietary supplements that contained the stuff. But here was the hitch: Those supplements contain Mickey Mouse amounts of the substance, whereas the laboratory mice were given such massive amounts that you and I would have to drink *hundreds of bottles* of red wine a day to get the same effect. Skoal.

But help may be coming in pill form. From anti-aging genes may come anti-aging drugs, the magic potion incarnate.

Dr. David Sinclair, a molecular biologist, is the professor who led the Harvard Medical School study on mice. He and others also founded a biomedical company that began working, doubtless as fast as it could, to develop a pill that would mimic the effects of caloric restriction. (A number of distinguished researchers in memory and aging have started such companies, and the competition, as you can imagine, is not sedate. Most of them have backing from major pharmaceutical houses. "If you don't do it," one of them told me, not for attribution, "you just can't stay in the game.")

A year before the mouse report was published, Dr. Sinclair had talked in a television interview about his team's study of aging in worms and fruit flies:

"The same genes that we're finding that extend life span in these simple organisms are found in people . . . We don't know if these are the key to longevity in people yet, but certainly they are the key to longevity in simple organisms." Then he said: "We're at the point where we need to test this first of all in mice . . . and if that works, we really want to go either into humans, if it's safe, or to try it in primates as well. But we're at the point where we are in mammals and we'll know within a year or two if we're right about this."

It took just one year to know, at least with mice, that they were right.

I asked him, "You have said, 'The goal is to see eventually that an eighty-year-old feels like a fifty-year-old does today.' Would this apply to memory? Could CR, or a pill to mimic CR, protect against normal memory loss?"

He said, "There's a reasonable chance that it could maintain memory through a lifetime. We see that neurons are protected against dying when you treat them with resveratrol or caloric restriction. Many molecules that work in mice don't work in humans, but we see no theoretical reason why it would work differently in humans."

It is an unwritten rule in the scientific community that the findings of any laboratory experiment must be confirmed by at least one other laboratory before being accepted. At the same time as Dr. Sinclair's study was published, there was another from France, led by Dr. Johan Auwerx of the Institute of Genetics and Molecular and Cellular Biology. It showed that mice fed resveratrol could out-perform other mice on the treadmill, two to one. "Resveratrol makes you look like a trained athlete without the training," Dr. Auwerx said.

The Sinclair team is working on developing molecules a thousand times more active than resveratrol. Dr. Sinclair himself had been taking resveratrol for several years, though he would not say in what form. He did say that his wife and parents had taken it, too, and half the workers in his lab. An act of faith, given that there was not yet any knowledge about potential side effects or what the long-range picture might be.

It almost didn't matter. Those reports about the mouse studies immediately generated a deafening buzz. Sales of over-the-counter dietary supplements containing resveratrol jumped tenfold overnight. The work of the Sinclair team was hailed by other researchers. There was even talk, *sotto voce* and some not so *sotto voce,* of Nobel Prizes, shimmering like visions of sugarplums in the air.

And maybe it would all happen. But in the sciences, many a sugarplum has turned into a prune. The closets are packed with reports of experiments that worked brilliantly — on mice. On humans, not so good. And also with remedies that *seemed* to work brilliantly on humans — until they didn't.

Think back to ephedra, the magic potion for weight loss, until it turned out that it might also be causing heart attacks and strokes. Think of torcetrapib, a drug that looked wonderfully promising for heart disease, until it was linked to deaths and coronary problems. Think, for heaven's sake, of the roller-coaster ride that women took for years on hormone replacement therapy. Finally, in 2002, came a major study that tied it to increased risk of breast cancer, and women in droves stopped taking hormones. By the very next year, breast-cancer rates had turned sharply downward for the first time in sixty years.

So much for sugarplums.

So if the promise of resveratrol, too, were to end up nowhere, what would we know for sure about diet and memory?

Rephrased: What does a Harvard School of Public Health professor of nutrition put down his own gullet for the health of his brain? Any supplements?

"A multivitamin," says Dr. Stampfer, "plus, during the winter months, a separate vitamin D supplement."

And in the department of food: What does he eat for dinner?

"Lots of fruits and vegetables. Rarely red meat. Fish several times a week."

For breakfast?

"Leftovers from dinner."

Of course. And for lunch?

"Peanut butter on whole-grain bread. Fruit. Chocolate."

Chocolate! Oh, yes, I say, I've seen it listed on Web sites as a brain food.

"I hope it's true," he says.

Grabs no headlines, got no glamour, got no buzz. But in the enduring absence of a magic potion, it is (excepting the Diet from Hell) the one true thing.

And I do love the part about the chocolate.

Chapter Fourteen:
It's All in the
Computer. Isn't it?

"Why does the computer analogy persist? Because they don't have another one."
— Dr. Terrence Deacon, professor of biological anthropology, University of California, Berkeley

"The disk is full," we say. And "There's just no more room on my hard drive." And "What I need is an upgrade."

Computer/brain: It has become one of the defining analogies of our time and our place and our state of mind, we tip-of-the-tonguers. But as analogies go, is it any good?

A friend tells me: "What drives me crazy is, it's in there, I *know* it's somewhere in there, like it is in the computer . . . but I just can't find it."

I ask, "How can you be sure it's in there?"

"Well, I guess I can't be absolutely sure, really. But I suspect it *must* be there, because it *was* there."

If human memory is like computer memory, everything we ever put into it should still be there. Everything, just as it was in the mind of that poor wretch Funes, the fictional character we met in Chapter Three, whose curse was that he could never forget a damned thing. Funes, who had total recall of every experience he had ever had, every single thing he had ever learned or heard or felt or smelled or seen, "every leaf of every tree," as his creator Jorge Luis Borges wrote. It should all be sitting in there, somewhere, waiting to be retrieved, unless we deliberately (or inadvertently, as I have done many a disastrous time at my computer) hit the Delete key. If we can't retrieve some particular tidbit of memory, it is not because it isn't there. It is simply because we haven't hit the right key — found the right retrieval cue.

According to this view, the human brain is a hard drive with its own rules of operation and its own software programs. The essential difference is simply, if you can imagine this as a *simply,* that it uses brain cells instead of chips and wires. In theory, it should be possible to construct a computer that would remember exactly as the brain remembers. When — not *if,* but *when* — we are able to understand fully how human memory works, that theory will become a reality.

Some psychologists and cognitive scientists embrace this view, and some philosophers, too. Computer scientists, of course, embrace it passionately.

Many neuroscientists do not go for it at all.

Everyone agrees that comparing the computer to the human brain is reasonable in certain basic respects: They are both systems of input and output. They take information in, they manipulate it, they store it, and they put it out. They both have incredible memories. Scientists can make many such technology/neurology equations. But for us, forever chasing lost items through the labyrinths of our brains, the big question stands: Is everything that went in there still there, computer-like, or isn't it?

The definitive answer: Nobody is sure.

Just as with the value of dietary supplements, the jury is still out. On this one, the jury may stay out. Nobody has been able to prove that everything that we ever put into memory is still there, and certainly nobody has been able to prove that it isn't, and possibly nobody ever will. There being this slight problem, either way: How would you go about proving it?

Obviously, if you never paid enough attention in the first place to move it from short-term memory into long, it is not there. Never was. A prevailing view among neuroscientists is that if it did get into deep storage, some version of it may still be stored, but not in its original form.

Think again of how a single memory is formed: It is a barrage of chemical and electrical signals that travels through neural networks in an innumerable series of chain reactions. Every single memory, and every single retrieval of an old memory, creates it own pattern of signals, so that every time you have pulled it out and put it back into storage, the pattern has changed.

Even our most powerful memories have been modified in this way over the years. The longer you have lived, the more times you may have pulled out that memory, the greater the modification may be. And it is altogether possible that if a memory has lain idle for long enough, without being retrieved at all, that particular pattern of signals has simply faded away. The old Use it or lose it, neurologically expressed.

The University of California biological anthropologist Terrence Deacon, well known for his work on the evolution of language and author of the book *The Sym-*

bolic Species: The Co-evolution of Language and the Brain, is not fond of the computer analogy.

"We tend to think of biology as we think of machines," he said when we met one afternoon at his home near the Berkeley campus. "We use machine metaphors to think about the brain because those are the metaphors that are easiest to talk about and easiest to communicate. But it's completely misleading. The way we remember things is totally different from writing on a disk or storing something on a memory chip. In those systems, all the details *are there.* However it went in, it stays that way. For us, it's just the opposite.

"I think of memory as a kind of palimpsest process, writing over something again and again and again." (Palimpsest, according to the dictionary: "a parchment, tablet, etc., that has been written upon or inscribed two or three times, the previous text or texts having been imperfectly erased") "So is everything in there that was there? It might be, but not in the way we would think about it. Because whenever we remember something, we are typically overlaying it on top of other memories."

It is not well understood, Dr. Deacon said, how we manage to get back through the layers of that palimpsest to find what's underneath. To keep the writing analogy, the ink is best when we're young. "And even though we write over it again and again and again, the stuff we write over it with is sort of in lighter ink. So when we try to go back, we can easily get it confused with the earlier stuff. The real surprise — I think it's a miracle — is that we're capable of going back at all. Say somebody recalls something that both of us saw a year ago, and I say that I just don't remember it. But if there are two or three other people who were with us at the time, and they all begin to add their parts of the memory, eventually I can recover it. I'll say, 'Oh, yeah — now I remember!' "

His palimpsest metaphor put me in mind of pentimento, another handy metaphor for memory. Literally, *pentimento* means that process by which images that have been painted over begin to show through the top layer of paint. Symbolically, it was used by the late Lillian Hellman as the title of her memoir, to describe past events of her life as they rose to the surface of consciousness through the layers of time.

There were critics who said that Hellman did an awful lot of fiddling with those events as they rose to the surface of consciousness through the layers of time — that her memory was *extremely* creative. (If you were watching late-night television in 1980, you may recall the brouhaha when the writer Mary McCarthy said on the *Dick Cavett Show,* "Every word she writes is a lie, including 'and' and 'the.' ") But the Hellman memoir made for gorgeous reading. And, besides, whose memories are not a bit creative?

"The brain operates by a very different logic from the computer. I think the palimpsest idea is a way to get people to understand that logic," Dr. Deacon said. "With a computer, the place where something is stored is the absolutely critical thing: I know that on this chip there are a million little bits stored in memory, and each one has a distinct, unique address. And whenever I need to retrieve one, I go back to the very same address."

"And we have no analogy to that?" I asked.

"*No* analogy. Our memories are not stored in some separate box in the brain that's for 'memories.' A human memory is stored in fragments. There is the visual part of it, there is the auditory part of it, there are the tactile and the motor and the emotional parts of it. There are all these components, and they're not stored in the same place. So what that means is, to get back to that memory, you need to get different bits of it hinted to you, different clues from all these fragments.

"But we have something extra: language. We can create a story, a narrative, to work our way back to the memory. For instance, I might ask you what you had for breakfast yesterday. Off the top of your head it might be difficult for you to come up with, but by constructing the story backward . . ."

"How would I do that?"

"Well, for myself, it might be: What did I do yesterday? Let's see, it was the day after Labor Day. Was my wife here, or had she already left? Did we have time to cook breakfast? No, we didn't. She had left, I can see her leaving. Okay, so what kind of breakfast would I have had? I usually have toast and coffee and juice. But that just didn't attract me. *Now* I remember. I had cereal, and now I can even remember what kind of cereal it was and how it smelled and how I mixed it. But thirty seconds ago, I couldn't have remembered any of that."

Theorists also have used the analogy of a river carving out a channel. It's a nice one, easy to grasp: The more times water flows down that channel, the deeper it will become. If it is carved deep enough, the water will never run outside it. That, in effect, is the formation of procedural memory — the implicit, unconscious, walking, talking, tying-your-shoelaces kind of memory.

But the question of what Dr. Deacon had for breakfast — no deep channel there. That belongs to episodic memory — personal, explicit, conscious, the kind that begins to lose speed with age. Tens of thousands of different breakfasts in each of our lives, and each one is a separate episodic memory, stored in various parts of the brain. How can we possibly make our way back to it?

Instead of one deep channel, Dr. Deacon says, picture rivulets. A large number of shallow little streams. Different bits of that memory of that particular breakfast are stored in different rivulets.

"This one is motor, this one is sensory, this one had to do with a particular sound or shape . . . and if you can get enough of them running, they resonate with each other. They are compatriots, so to speak. So if a couple of them get going, they increase the probability that others that were carved at the same time, in the same situation, will also get going — and you will remember."

Which gives us some sense of what is happening biologically when we remember by association: all those compatriot fragments rallying each other along, to reach a goal called What I Had for Breakfast Yesterday.

This kind of associating is what our brains do wonderfully well. This is what computers do not do so well. This is what futurists will assure you (see Chapter Seventeen) that the computers of tomorrow will do very well indeed — *at least* as well as our brains.

But in our own moment, in a contest between computer memory and human memory — not just memory belonging to a human of a certain age but *any* human memory — which would prevail?

It depends, really, on the terms of the contest. Speed? Precision? Creative approach?

Specialists agree that these are the main differences between the two:

1. Methods of encoding information
2. Speed
3. Accuracy

Each has its strengths and weaknesses.

First, and most important, are the different ways computers and humans take in information.

The computer, being digital, works step by step, while the brain, being built more along analog lines, works in a continuum.

If you do not understand what this means, you will not learn it from me. The reason you will not learn it from me is that I do not understand it either. Not *really,* not technologically.

I do know that the vocabulary of digital is all zeros and ones, nothing more, and from these it builds universes of information. This gave me trouble until it occurred to me that Morse code also manages to say a mouthful, and does it with nothing more than dots and dashes. Not that Morse code is digital, but it does help me grasp the *nature* of the thing, if not the technology.

As to analog, I was greatly helped by this suggestion from the New York University professor of mathematics Harold Edwards: "Think of analog in terms of the volume knob on a radio," he said. "You turn it up, you turn it down, it is a *continuum.*"

So between the dots and dashes and the radio volume I feel better about the whole thing, and if you also have trouble on this plane of reality, maybe you will feel better, too.

Fortunately, it is not always necessary to understand how things work in order to use them. To wit: How many of us *really* understand how electricity works, or gravity or aspirin or (for that matter) that volume knob on the radio? Which does not keep us from making good use of all of them.

Now, as to speed: "A two-gigaherz machine" (and don't even ask me what that means) "is doing hundreds of millions of operations a second," the Johns Hopkins neurologist Barry Gordon tells me. "It is *insanely* fast; it is doing an amazing number of things — although they are simple things, like moving a bit from one spot to another — but it is doing them one at a time.

"By contrast, the hundred billion or more neurons in my head work vastly slower, only on the order of ten times per second. But the brain's machinery is doing hundreds of things at once. When you walk and talk, for example, you are doing two separate things, involving very different systems, but simultaneously. While you are writing, your visual system is also paying attention to what is happening in the periphery of your vision. If a bug were to crawl on the window shade, you would react." You bet I would. "These are two of the major differences: the vast difference in relative operating rates of the computer and the brain, and the computer's serial operation versus the parallel operation of the brain — though there are now computers that do have some parallel operations. That gap is narrowing."

And accuracy?

Here, he says, the computer has two big advantages: the fact that it finds by address, and its exactitude:

"If I were a computer and I wanted to locate you, I would have to know your exact address, and that is where you would be. If I don't know the address, I can't find you. That is how computer memory works: It's one or zero, there or not there, yes or no. So the information can be transmitted without error. Now, if I were doing it associatively, I wouldn't have to know exactly where you live. I would stand in the street and shout, 'Martha,' and all the Marthas would turn their heads. The sound would find you. But some Marcias or Martins might think, 'Did I just hear my name called?' and they might respond, too. So there would be that ambiguity. That's how our memory works — not by location but by similar characteristics."

You may recall that Sherlock Holmes, a genius of associative memory — who didn't care to know anything about the solar system because it would only clutter up his brain — compared human memory to an attic that must be kept orderly. We can keep our computer files orderly by organizing them efficiently (not that I do, but we *can*). If they become overcrowded or are no longer relevant, we can clear them out. We delete them.

What about brains, then? The longer we live, the more numerous and crowded and layered our memories become, the more they may interfere with one another. How can we clear out a brain?

We can't, Dr. Gordon says. We don't really erase anything. What we do, in effect, is write over it. "But you *can* keep unnecessary things in that attic, if you just organize them properly.

"We call it the paradox of experts: Experts know a lot, and memories interfere with each other, so all that expert knowledge should cause a lot more clutter and interference in their brains. But it doesn't, because they organize that information." (The paradox has pedigree. The statesman Marcus Tullius Cicero said sometime in the first century B.C. that the best help to memory was not mnemonics but *order.* Not my strong suit.)

"Take bird watchers: They say, Oh, there's a bird with a beak and long legs, and it's flightless. That belongs in this category. Raptors go over there, eagles and vultures go together over here . . . They categorize everything they see; everything gets slotted into its place."

It is akin to the so-called loci system, formally called the *method of loci,* which is one of the oldest and best-known mnemonic techniques in recorded history. The legend, and maybe even the fact, is that it was invented in the fifth century B.C. by the Greek poet Simonides. Professional mnemonists use it when they perform that neat trick of asking a hundred audience members to stand up and call out their names, and then the pro calls back the names in order. Maybe even backward, to really knock 'em dead.

It is done by visual association. Say you need to make a string of telephone calls, to Tina, Tom, Dick, Harry, Mary, and Jane. You visualize each of them in a different room of some familiar location, such as your home. You picture your living room full of Tinas, your dining room crowded with Toms, the kitchen mobbed with Dicks, the bedroom packed with Marys, the den with Harrys, and the guest room (you have a nice-size home; if you don't, you need a different mnemonic) with Janes. When you want to remember the string of telephone calls, you take a mental stroll through the rooms, and there they are. Hopefully. (What fascinates me about this 2,700-year-old trick is that it seems, in a way, to presage computers: Find by location.)

Few of us have any pressing need to recite a hundred names backward, but the system actually works quite well for modest memory tasks: You picture your bed piled high with stuff that needs to go to the cleaners, your kitchen table covered with bills that need to be paid . . . or, as I have said before and do not hesitate to say again, you can always make a list.

So human memory cannot delete, which I think is really too bad, but it can straighten out the mess. Can it save?

"Probably the hippocampal system does that," Dr. Gordon said.

Can it make backup files?

"Not in the sense used in computers, but we have automatic backup files in terms of multiple encodings of our memories and multiple storage sites."

Can its capacity, like the computer's, be upgraded?

On this occasion we were talking by telephone, but he must have been smiling.

"The capacity of our memory," he said, "has been getting upgraded for six million years."

■ ■ ■ ■

So the computer remembers all or nothing. No in-between. Whereas the brain is filled with in-between. Think of it this way: What you put into the computer is an abstraction of your experience. Retrieve it, and it's unchanged. What you *remember* is an abstraction of that experience, then a reconstruction of the abstraction, then a reconstruction of the reconstruction, and so on and on and on — every time you retrieve it. And, of course, the more time that passes, the truer this becomes.

In the grand old movie musical *Gigi,* there was a honey of a duet called "I Remember It Well." It was sung by Maurice Chevalier and Hermione Gingold, both long gone now, as a pair of seniors recalling a brief romantic fling from their youth.

Nostalgically, he sings of their carriage ride home. No, no, Gingold sings in her memorable growl, "You walked me home."

He remembers that she lost a glove. No, she says, it was a comb.

He recalls the brilliance of the sky; she recalls rain.

He recalls the Russian songs they heard, and she that they were songs from Spain.

Yes! he croons, his eyes glittering at the memory. "Ah, yes, I remember it well."

Which illustrates what Harvard's Dr. Daniel L. Schacter means when he speaks of the *reproductive* memory of the computer versus the *constructive* memory of our brains.

That memory of the man's — that is constructive memory, repeatedly *re*constructed over the years. And maybe the woman's is too, for all we know — maybe it was snowing and she actually lost a scarf — although it is the conceit of the song that her memory is accurate *because women remember such things.*

But if it had all been entered into a computer and saved when it happened, and retrieved ten, twenty, a hundred years later, the weather report and the lost-and-found notes would still be there, reproduced precisely as entered. That is reproductive memory.

Brain memory has emotion. The computer is one cold fish. Suppose you recall some major personal event — tragic, terrifying, delightful, whatever. Whenever you pull out that memory, its details will be subtly altered by your recollection of grief or terror or delight, as well as by the muting effects of time.

If you had entered the experience in your computer immediately after it happened, and retrieved it years later, your memory might have changed so much that you would look at the screen with wonder, thinking, "But that's not how I recall it at all!" just as we sometimes do when we see pictures of ourselves as children and say, "Is that really me? I don't feel as though I was ever that child!"

And here is the big question: The cold fish remembers precisely, but does it *know* that it remembers?

After World War II, the British mathematician Alan Mathison Turing worked on the design of what he called universal automatic computing machines. He developed a tricky exercise that came to be known as the Turing test. The test was said to be inspired by a then-popular party game called the Imitation Game, which went like this:

Two of the party, a man and a woman, are in separate rooms, unseen by the others. The other guests ask them questions and the man and the woman send back typewritten answers. The aim of these two is to convince the gathering that they are each other, and the aim of the gathering is to figure out which is which. (Since the logic on both sides would depend heavily on stereotypical thinking about gender, you can understand why this game might not go over too well today.)

Turing proposed a twist on the game: Instead of a man and a woman, the subjects are a human and a computer. There is a human observer who does not see the subjects, does not know which is which, and proceeds to ask them questions. If the observer keeps asking and asking, probing hard, and still cannot tell which is which, the computer wins.

Turing anticipated objections to his test (there were many) and provided his own answers, such as:

"Heads in the Sand objection: The consequences of machines' thinking would be too dreadful. Let us hope and believe that they cannot do so."

Answer: That is a moral argument, Turing said in effect, not a scientific one.

Theological objection: Since thinking is a function of the immortal human soul, there is no way a computer could possibly think.

Answer: If God wanted to give the computer a soul, God could certainly do so.

Thus far, no computer has won. Thus far.

If a computer did win that test, the inescapable inference would be that machines can think.

Many specialists believe that this is where the brain-computer analogy falls apart. To think, after all, presupposes an "I." Whenever and whatever we remember, there is an "I" doing the remembering. That "I" has the *sensation* of remembering — and also the sensation of possession. You know that *your* memory is not somebody else's. You have the conscious awareness that it belongs to *you.*

Even more dramatic, if you are, say, sixty years old, you know that your *memory* of a *memory* of something that happened *a half century ago* belongs, beyond all possible doubt, to you. (Which only *sounds* elementary. When we consider what it takes to get us from here to there — instantly! — in the neuronal cosmos of our brains, it is, as Dr. Deacon says, a miracle.)

By this standard, there is no question of who wins a computer-brain contest. There is no contest. Computers have no "I." (To which the futurists say, Just you wait. But we will get to that later.)

It is a nice thing to have an "I." I am extremely happy to have one. But the price we pay for the "I" is the imprecision of our memories; and I could not imagine, until I put the question to Dr. Schacter, what the practical advantage of an imprecise memory might be.

We talked in his office near Harvard Yard. "One reason why memory has this constructive character, and why it's not a rote repetition of the past, may be that a system that works this way is more advantageous for planning for the future," he said. "If you can be flexible in how you remember the past, or combine elements of different experiences from the past, it would help you anticipate what's going to happen in the future. Because the future, of course, is never going to be an exact repetition of the past."

He makes this distinction: The computer is a repository of knowledge, whereas the brain is a rememberer of experience. The computer does not need to plan for future situations that might be different from past situations. The brain does. So the brain has to deal with some exceedingly different problems from those of the standard computer.

"God help us if we had computers that worked like brains and gave us back the *gist* instead of the exact file that we put in. We don't want the gist from the computer, we want the exact thing. It isn't involved in inferring what *might* have happened, based on fragmentary information. It's literal. And that's great for the computer, but that's not our system, and we wouldn't want it to be."

Dr. Schacter speaks of memory as a form of "mental time travel." The phrase perfectly captures one of the associative marvels of our memories. I have an example from just several nights ago:

I was in a restaurant in New York and ate roast beef, which brought me directly to the memory of a restaurant in London where I had eaten superb roast beef six years ago, which then reminded me of a friend who now lives in London, whom I used to see frequently at a beach on Cape Cod, way back in the nineteen seventies, and from there I was transported instantly to rapturous summer weekends at various beaches with my parents and my brother, much further back, in the nineteen forties.

So within seconds, I had traveled across six decades and a remarkably broad swath of territory — geographically, gustatorily (in that department, my memory is fine), emotionally, every which way.

The computer that can do that does not exist. Nobody can say that it *will* not. (In his book, Dr. Schacter gracefully hedges the bet: "Whether the gulf that separates the two is entirely and forever impassable remains to be seen.") But it *does* not.

And then we come to that other, ultimate marvel of human memory, which is its creativity.

Our ability to create, to imagine, to fantasize, flows directly out of our ability to associate — and this does not fade with age.

The brain does all this automatically. The computer must look things up. True, it does so with a terrible, wonderful swiftness. But for all its speed, it does not soar.

"What does a computer lack that a person has?" a *New York Times* reporter asked the Indiana University cognitive scientist Douglas Hofstadter.

"It has no concepts," he replied.

The reporter then said, "I know some people who have no concepts," and Hofstadter answered — quite wonderfully, I thought: "They do have concepts. People are filled to the brim with concepts. You don't have to know what a concept is in order to have one."

It takes the human brain to play around with past experience, to pull it apart and put it together again in a thousand different ways, creating a thousand different story lines out of fragments of memory. It takes the brain to poke through its own imperfect files, experimenting with innumerable combinations of fragments, arriving finally at some combination that gives full pleasure to the senses, adding a pinch of this and a dash of that, sort of like a good chef ad-libbing a soup, and end up not with a soup but a poem.

Of course, the production of a *good* poem is rare. But the glory of human memory is that it can produce one at all — and that any one of us, at any age, can give it a try.

So if you want swift, brilliant, 100 percent reliable accuracy, go for computer memory.

If you want imagination, creativity, hit-or-miss, out-of-the-box, off-the-wall combinations of tangerines and apples, just possibly to put together such a wonder of a tapple as the world has never seen — if you want *that,* go for brain memory.

At least, that's what you should go for today. Tomorrow could be another story.

Chapter Fifteen: Flashbulb Memories

WHERE WERE YOU WHEN . . . ?

"September Eleventh?" said Giorgio Marchetti, a businessman from Italy. "I remember it exactly, *exactly.* I am pilot, not for working but for pleasure, and this day I fly back home to Milano from Lugano in Switzerland. I landed the plane and go in the building and I see nobody. No police, no inspectors for passports, no other people, nobody! I am surprised, because in my country, when we come back from another country, we must present the passport, even if we are Italians.

"I was thinking, What has happened here? Then I saw in one place a big crowd, with the policemen and everybody, and they are all standing and looking at a television screen. And I went and say to somebody, 'What is happening?' Then I saw. And everyone was standing in a silence, a terrible silence, like a shock. To the end of my life I will always hear this silence. It is a big surprise to me, how much clear are this silence and these pictures of this day in my mind."

Flashbulb memories, psychologists call them: the memories of where we were and what we were doing at the instant we learned of some momentous event.

Where were you when you got word of 9/11? Where were you when you heard that John F. Kennedy had been shot? Or Martin Luther King or Bobby Kennedy or Lee Harvey Oswald? Or when the *Challenger* exploded? Or when you heard that a princess had crashed into eternity in a Paris tunnel or that men had landed on the moon . . . Where were you? The scenes sit like pictures in the mind's eye.

And the precision of these pictures! People remember not only where they were and how they heard but also whom they were with, what they were doing, what they were saying, thinking, eating . . . Ask, and they say, "Oh, I remember *exactly.*" That is everyone's refrain. The Kennedy assassination, in 1963: "I remember *exactly.*" Boomers who were then in grade school: "I remember *exactly.*" Octogenarians who were then raising the boomers: "I remember *exactly.*"

We are now in territory where routine

memory problems are — forgive me — *no problem.* How to forget, that's the trick.

Flashbulb memory resists the incursions of age, and the reasons hold a crucial lesson for us all.

The kind of memory the flashbulb most closely resembles is the memory of deeply personal experience, like those childhood traumas that also are resistant to age. Like those others, flashbulb memories have a powerful photographic quality: We *see* them. And like those others, flashbulb memories are tenacious. They are the clinging vines of memory. People say that these are among the most vivid memories of their lives — as vivid as their memories of the most important personal events.

But here is the oddity: These are *not* personal events. They are as public as public can get. And yet, we seem to encode them as personal experience.

The psychologist Ulric Neisser has said: "The flashbulb recalls an occasion when two narratives that we ordinarily keep separate — the course of history and the course of our own life — were momentarily put into alignment."

Two narratives. Two memory systems. You remember (I hope) reading earlier about different kinds of memory. Semantic memory is facts. (Fact: John F. Kennedy was killed in Dallas.) Episodic memory is personal experience. (Personal experience: "I was just going out the school door when I heard someone yelling something about President Kennedy.")

This is where the two kinds of memory seem to fuse, just as personal and communal identities seem to fuse. We are part of the public experience and the public experience is part of us, and just try to separate the two.

Test it out: If you are old enough to remember the scene, try to recall that iconic image of the child John-John saluting his father's coffin, his mother standing veiled and vacant-eyed behind him, without recalling your own emotions.

I have interviewed scores of people, from here and abroad, asking what they remember of those precise moments, on September 11, 2001, and on November 22, 1963, when they first heard the news.

After a time, common threads emerge. When they talk about the day the World Trade towers came down, many of them recall, alongside the horror, the ominous signs and portents that help would not be needed.

It was like that for the author-educator Joel Conarroe and for the lawyer Ellyn Polshek, each of whom lived in Greenwich Village, within sight of the disaster.

CONARROE: I was in the roof garden of my building when a plane flew alarmingly low overhead and then hit the first tower. I saw the second plane hit. People were on balconies and decks everywhere, and when the first building collapsed we all screamed. I still hear that eerie chorus . . . When I finally left the building there was a line, snaking around the corner from St. Vincent's Hospital for several blocks, of people waiting to give blood.

POLSHEK: I was on the treadmill watching CNN. A reporter said that a plane had just hit the World Trade. She said it must be "a glitch." They showed the tower with fire pouring out. Then I saw another plane. My first thought was, "Wow, the authorities are fast, sending it to inspect the damage." It flew behind the tower, then I saw a brilliant flash . . . A workman in the apartment watched with me. He kept saying, "This is the third world war." I remember the triage doctors waiting outside St. Vincent's. They stood there alone most of the day.

It was like that for Mary Willis, a New York writer:

I was in the kitchen and my sister called and said, "Turn on the TV." I turned it on just as the second plane hit. I immediately went down to the Red Cross and gave blood — which, of course, they didn't need. But no one knew it yet.

And it was like that for my husband and me, and who knows how many of our neighbors, rushing across Central Park to the nearest hospital, to give whatever help would surely be required. Instead we found dozens of aides standing silently outside the hospital, waiting for the ambulances that never arrived.

Then, later but just as indelible, come the afterimages:

The day after 9/11, Bob and I were taken down to Ground Zero and driven around the site. We stopped at an open area. I will never forget seeing three crossed steel beams which had landed in that area, like three crosses, and policemen and workers on their knees, praying to them.

— Ina Caro, historian, New York

A week after the president was assassinated, our family was out driving when a tire on a passing car suddenly gave out. It sounded like a shot. Susie, who was then five, screamed, "Duck, Daddy!" I suppose that to a child's mind, important men were now a target. And who could be more important than this little kid's own father?
— Maggie Scarf, writer, New Haven, Connecticut

Why do flashbulb memories endure in this vivid, pictorial way?

In part, simply and obviously, because of their emotional force. Just as happens with those urgent personal experiences, the amygdala, the brain's mediator of emotion, is working full blast, carving the memory deep.

But also — and for us, this is the key point — we remember flashbulb events so well because we rehearse them. Endlessly.

It is just as all the memory specialists keep telling us: What makes a memory stick is to rehearse it, form associations with it, elaborate on it, involve all the senses. And with these flashbulb events, we do involve the senses to some nth degree. Indeed, we cannot help ourselves. Thinking of them; dreaming of them; repeating to each other, incalculable times, the details of just where we were and just what we were doing when we heard the news . . . and the nonstop press coverage, the inescapable television images shown again and again and again for weeks, for months, and yet again on every anniversary . . . Talk about rehearsal time! If we ever required proof of the role of repetition and elaboration in memory, flashbulb memories, alas, will provide it.

It is a hell of a way to be given proof. Spare us such memories, spare us such proof. But here's the point: Whether the event is shocking or humdrum, the *process* is the same. It is committed to memory by elaboration.

If the event is shocking, the memory is encoded automatically. If it is humdrum, we have to apply a little elbow grease. To remember those banalities that drive us wacko — the *Whatsisname?* and the *Who told me that?* and the *When was I there?* and the *What was I saying?* and the *Why did I come into this room?* and, of course, the ever-popular *Where did I leave my glasses?* — to remember those takes elaboration. It takes repetition, repetition, and — at risk of repeating myself — repetition.

It used to be thought that flashbulb memory

was somehow unique. The term itself was introduced in the seventies by two psychologists, Roger Brown and James Kulick, who believed that a flashbulb moment sets off some special neurological process that fires like a camera's flash to preserve the image in the brain. That's what gives it that uncanny pictorial quality. *Now Print,* they called it.

They interviewed dozens of people about their memories of the murders of the Kennedy brothers and Martin Luther King.

Half the interviewees were black and half were white. All but one had flashbulb memories of the attack on JFK. (Remember, we are not talking about general memory of the event, but memory of the specific moment of *learning* about the event.) About half had flashbulb memories of the attack on Robert Kennedy. And of the attack on Martin Luther King? Three-quarters of the blacks remembered — and one-third of the whites.

Given those compelling results, the psychologists concluded that the more relevance a public event has *for the individual,* the more likely that the Now Print mechanism will fire.

Most researchers no longer believe in the Now Print. They believe that what happens on the neurological level is probably the same as what happens with powerful personal memories: The flashbulb memory is fixed by its emotional significance and by repeated rehearsal.

This explains why these memories are so little affected by age. When I asked people where they were and what they were doing when they first heard about the attacks on the World Trade Center, the eighty-year-olds answered with just as much clarity and detail as the forty-year-olds.

Katie Popper, a cookbook author, recalled with precision:

I was on my way to the beauty parlor, on the number ten bus. The driver announced that something bad had happened downtown and we would be rerouted. We didn't know what it was, but I figured that if something terrible had happened, I'd better get food. So I got off the bus and went to a supermarket and loaded up with two heavy bags and then tried to get a cab home. But by that time there were no cabs. No buses, no subways, nothing was moving. Just great mobs of people silently walking up Broadway from downtown.

Katie Popper is ninety-three.

In short, what mattered — what always matters in flashbulb memories — was not how old people were but how much emotional freight the event held for them. In this arena, at least, emotion trumps age.

This also explains why people in other countries, such as Giorgio Marchetti from Italy, whom I quoted earlier, and the author-composer Elmer Schönberger, a friend in Amsterdam, whom I quote now, have such powerful flashbulb memories of an event that took place in America:

> I was at home, working. I was going that night to a terrific concert program in the Amsterdam Concertgebouw, with *De Staat* of Louis Andriessen, a work that means more to me than any other Dutch music from the last half century. When I work at home the world more or less stops to exist for me. Why did I turn on the television set that afternoon? I don't know. I know only that from that very moment on, a few minutes before the second tower was to be hit, I have been glued to the screen. Ever since, *De Staat* is the piece which I did *not* hear on the night of 9/11.

And Manuel Montesinos, a foundation executive in Madrid:

I came home for lunch about two thirty Madrid time. I poured myself a glass of good Ríoja red wine and was helping to set the table. When I turned on the television, we were sitting down to the table. They were repeating the attack of the first plane. There were as yet no news about who could have been behind the attack. But since there are moments of great violence in the United States, produced by sick people, my first thought was it must be some suicidal maniac.

I did not ask them, but I doubt that they would have flashbulb memories of President Kennedy's murder, any more than we would have flashbulb memories of the Berlin Wall coming down in 1989, although my German friends certainly do, or that we would have flashbulb memories of the assassination of the Swedish prime minister Olof Palme in 1986 — although Swedes certainly do. The killing of an American president, however shocking, was of no personal significance to most non-Americans. September eleventh was.

Most of the Americans whom I interviewed are boomer age, and they have all the usual memory complaints. But ask them where they were when they heard about

JFK, and *wham.* You could write a play, you could cast it and stage it and design the set and lay in the props, with the richness of detail in their memories.

Youth, of course, would be especially susceptible to high emotion. All those hormones flowing, all that adrenaline flooding the system, carving ever deeper into the memory channels of the brain.

"We were milling around during a break between classes when they announced over the loudspeaker that President Kennedy had been shot. We were asked to come immediately to the auditorium," recalled Betsy Burton, who owns a bookstore in Salt Lake City. "All the kids who had been fighting their way through the halls in various directions turned as one body toward the auditorium. We all moved slowly forward. We felt a need to whisper. I can still see the faces of the friends I was walking with quite vividly, as if I were seeing them on a screen.

"The principal told us what had occurred. That instant, and the faces of my friends in the hall when the announcement came — they are scenes that I can replay in Technicolor."

"I was in English class in Chevy Chase, Maryland. I remember that the principal came into the classroom and lowered the blinds. We were sent home early. I remember that my mother made pasta and when she drained it, she dumped it into the drain of the sink without a strainer, because she didn't think what she was doing. She was crying." This is Katie Moffitt, a ceramicist from Princeton, New Jersey. Consider the detail. Moffitt is fifty-eight years old. She was fourteen when it happened. Carried in her mind's eye over a span of forty-four years is the lowered blind, the missing strainer, the pasta plugging the drain of the sink.

Consider this, too: If you are old enough to remember 1963, how much else do you remember, in any detail at all, from that year? Or, for that matter, from 2001?

Here is another curious feature of the flashbulb: It inspires our unshakable conviction that our memory is accurate.

Jeremy Pikser, a screenwriter from New York, recalled the Kennedy killing in cinematic detail:

I was working with some of my fellow junior-high students, decorating the gym for a Thanksgiving dance. Someone said that someone else had said that the president had been shot. I went to the school office and found that it was true but that he was still alive. No one knew what to do, so we went on decorating until we heard that he was dead. The student council president said that he didn't see why we should cancel the dance. Everyone else thought he was crazy. On the way home I passed the yard of a girl with very bright red hair. She was from the South and a real JFK hater, but she was terribly shocked when I told her. I had not liked him either — but from the left — but I almost cried when I told her.

Then he said, "I'm really not certain how accurate any of this is. But what's interesting to me is, whether true or false, how clear and vivid the memory is."

That is interesting to me, too. Because, of all the people whom I asked, Where were you when? Pikser was the only one who suggested that his memory might be anything less than totally accurate.

We tend to preserve our flashbulbs under glass. We insist that we remember *exactly.* Challenge my memory of that book I read last week, and I'll say (maybe, if I'm feeling mellow), "Well, you know. My memory is terrible." Challenge my memory of how I heard that JFK had been shot, and I'll tell you that you weren't with me, so bug off.

But, in fact, *exactly* is not so exact. Flash-bulb memory is not perfect; it is simply much better than most. What has fascinated researchers is why we have such faith in its perfection.

Partly, of course, it is because of the enormous emotional investment that we have in such memories. We protect our investments. But the researchers have found that something else kicks in: Memory of that pivotal moment may be bent out of shape by whatever happened immediately *after* the moment.

For example, I interviewed a woman who insisted that she had been home alone, lying in bed and nursing a headache, when she heard about the shooting on the radio. Yet her husband was just as insistent that they had heard it together in the kitchen, that she had become increasingly upset with each subsequent bulletin, and finally had gone to lie down. He had left for his office and found her still lying down when he came home.

Probably — not *absolutely,* but probably — she had conflated the moment with its aftermath. As she rehearsed the event repeatedly over time, what had come to dominate her memory were those hours spent alone, in great agitation.

We are more likely to make such mistakes (if, in fact, it was a mistake; maybe the *husband* was misremembering!) as we get older, simply because we've had more rehearsal time. We have retrieved that flashbulb and put it back into storage, and retrieved it again and stored it again, layer upon layer upon layer of memory, and with each re-storing there is subtle alteration — not because of memory loss but because that's the way memory seems to work. (Extensive rehearsal time does have its downside. But then, what doesn't?)

So if others were with you on the occasion of a flashbulb event and now say of your recollection, "Nope, that's not how it was," do not bite their heads off. They may be right. On the other hand, *you* may be right, in which case it is okay to bite their heads off. I would.

In any event, this is, I assure you, the absolutely, precisely, exact way in which I heard that JFK had been shot:

I was on a publicity tour for my first book, an eminently forgettable book, and was waiting backstage on the morning of November 22, 1963, Los Angeles time, to appear on Art Linkletter's television show. Remember Art Linkletter?

It was early. The host had not yet arrived. The audience sat out front. I peeked between the curtains and saw that it was a full house. A crew member looked at a television monitor and promptly cried out. Then we all watched, standing there backstage, as the terrible story unfolded.

Linkletter arrived. His producer took him aside. I heard him say: "No, no, we'll do the show."

The designated warm-up man went out front to warm up the audience. I heard a shriek, and I thought, He has just told them what happened. But no, he had not told them what happened. He had told them who won the door prize.

I do not remember what the door prize was.

Linkletter then went out front and made the announcement, and there was a great communal exhalation of breath and then a profoundly stunned silence, and then the show went on.

Later, I wondered why I hadn't left. (But then, I was crazy about Kennedy. Let me not lay that on anyone who did not like him and did not mourn.)

I wondered why others hadn't left. Most probably, because people just don't know what to do. In such disordered moments there is an urgent countervailing impulse toward order, routine, continuity.

I wondered, as I often have in one circumstance or another, *Why* must the show go on? The only reasonable answer I ever heard was from a theater manager who said, "Because, if it doesn't, the box office has to return the receipts." Whoever said, "Follow the money" was on the money.

Then came my afterimage, and there, too, was the aura of money:

On November 22, my late husband joined me in Los Angeles, and on the 23rd we went to Las Vegas, where several press interviews had been arranged for me.

Las Vegas was silent. Las Vegas was surreal. Las Vegas was in mourning. There was a moratorium on gambling until 12:01 a.m. on November 24. The casinos were locked and the whole town looked to us like a sea of green, green baize cloths draped over the slot machines, the gaming tables, everything.

By 11 p.m., in our hotel lobby, a crowd had begun to form outside the closed casino doors.

By 11:45, the crowd was huge, loud, restive.

At 12:01 the doors were flung open and — here is my afterimage — the herd went thundering through like starvelings in some blighted land toward food being dropped from a helicopter. Shouting, shoving, elbowing each other. I still see them. I still hear an attendant yelling frantically, "Take it easy! Take it easy! Take it easy!"

Finally, a flashbulb memory from a woman who, understandably enough, insisted upon anonymity. She was the only one I interviewed who actually showed me corroboration of her story:

My parents were away, my kid brother was in school, and I played hooky and my boyfriend came over. We spent the whole morning in my bedroom, fooling around. *Heavy* petting. So we didn't have a clue what was going on in the world.

They let the kids out of school hours early. My brother came home and we never heard him. And suddenly there was this *flash,* and the little snot had taken our picture. He said — and I quote, these were his exact words — "You're disgusting. Turn on the TV." Then he ran out of the house and we pulled ourselves together and turned on the TV, and it was just in time to watch Walter Cronkite make that announcement, you know, "President Kennedy died at . . ." and then he took off his glasses and looked up at the clock. It was twelve something. I can still see him so clearly, taking off those glasses and putting them back on and trying not to cry . . .

My brother never told my parents. I knew he wouldn't. He was a good kid, even though we hated each other back then. For years I begged him for the picture, and he would never give it to me. Finally, almost ten years later, when I got engaged, he got it all giftwrapped and he gave it to me as an engagement gift.

I think of it — how could one not? — as the ultimate flashbulb memory.

Chapter Sixteen: The Big Picture

Why Did This Happen (to Me), Mr. Darwin?

Heigh-ho. Nature is a good mother if you are in your reproductive years and a bad stepmother — not wicked, simply indifferent — to the rest of us.

I would rather have wicked, in a way. Indifference is such an insult. But indifference, regrettably, is what makes sense. Since the whole point of her arduous exercise is reproduction, why should she do anything for us when we are no longer doing anything for her?

So she doesn't.

I was discussing this with Dr. William Jagust, the University of California, Berkeley neuroscientist, and his cat.

About this cat, named Teddy: He had been nuzzling, doggie style, at my feet in Dr. Jagust's study, then had leaped up onto the coffee table, right next to my tape recorder, and sat there silent, alert, seeming to take everything in as fully as the tape recorder itself. And though I am really more of a dog person, he seemed so attentive, so manifestly *happy* to be there, that it made me happy, too.

"Have you come across the term *antagonistic pleiotropy?*" Dr. Jagust asked amiably, the way one might ask Have you tried that hot new restaurant on Nob Hill?

I assured him that I had not. Neither he nor Teddy looked surprised.

"It's a very simple concept despite the name. It's the idea that a gene that is good for you at one stage in your life can have very deleterious consequences later — but those consequences are irrelevant. The best example is testosterone. Testosterone is very good if you're a male. It makes you strong, it makes you run fast, it's better for reproduction. But if you have it for a long period of time, you may get prostate cancer. It doesn't matter to evolution if you get prostate cancer in your fifties or sixties, as long as you were strong and healthy when you were twenty.

"That's antagonistic pleiotropy. A lot of what happens as we age is probably a manifestation of functions that were important in early life but are irrelevant in later life."

Seen in these evolutionary terms, certain

302

mysteries of memory take on other dimensions.

Mystery: Why should some kinds of memory stay strong while others weaken?

We know the biological answers — frontal lobes shrink, connections between neurons diminish in numbers and strength, and so forth — but what is the evolutionary reason? Is there a survival advantage? I.e., Mr. Darwin, where's the beef?

Mystery: names. Why do we forget them? We reviewed the obvious reasons in Chapter One: because names are words without meaning and such and so. But in evolutionary terms, *why?*

You may recall the *Just So Stories* which Rudyard Kipling is said to have written for the pleasure of his little daughter; maybe the tot actually hated them, but that is what is said. They were published in 1902, which means that they have been getting read to roughly four generations of children, perhaps including you and yours.

Just So stories answer questions such as these: Why does the leopard have spots? Why does the hippopotamus have such a tough hide? Why does the elephant have such a long nose? (Because, once upon a time, a baby elephant wandered away from home and got too close to the water's edge and a crocodile grabbed the baby elephant's nose in his mouth and tried to pull him into the stream and pulled and pulled and pulled . . . *Aha.* Just so.)

In reality, Just So's are hard to come by. For all the overwhelming evidence in support of Darwinian theory, there is also a lot of informed speculation — why we have developed this feature and that, what the survival advantages have been, and so forth — and some hugely informed specialists do not like to play those guessing games at all.

At the American Museum of Natural History, in Manhattan, Dr. Ian Tattersall is a curator in the Division of Anthropology, and the author of many books on human evolution, including *The Fossil Trail: How We Know What We Think We Know About Human Evolution.* (I love that *"Think We Know."* Great title.)

I asked him to look at normal memory loss through a Darwinian prism, and he politely begged off. "A lot of things happen randomly, for passive reasons," he said. "But we're a storytelling species. We love to have stories told to us, and many people are happy to oblige." And added, "People canonize Darwin, and freeze him, and he would have hated that. All science is provisional."

And it is true, of course, that we yearn for the Just So. We do not want provisional answers. We freeze Darwin because we want answers frozen in certainty, and often we cannot have them.

That said, scientists can make some extremely reasonable guesses, and typically they provide their own provisionals. Speaking with them, I have found it striking how, almost invariably, they will say, "Probably," and "We think," and "This is just my own theory, but . . ."

Come back to the good old antagonistic pleiotropy, and to Dr. Jagust's explanation: "A lot of what happens as we age is probably a manifestation of functions that were important in early life but are irrelevant in later life."

Probably it works pretty much like that with our memories. Take, for instance, that first mystery I posed: Why do some kinds of memory have more lasting power than others?

Procedural memory, which (if you remember) covers everything we do on automatic, and semantic memory, which covers facts, and episodic memory, which covers personal experience, are all strong when we are young adults. They have to be. We are no longer in the care of our parents;

we need to look after ourselves and our offspring; we need to be able to remember not only how to tie a shoe (procedural) and what a shoe is (semantic) but also when our shoes need repair and what size shoes to buy for the kids and where we could possibly have kicked off those shoes when we got home last night — all episodic.

Time passes. Procedural stays intact.

Semantic stays pretty good (you may momentarily forget what to call that stuff you like in your salad, but you know what arugula *is*).

Episodic begins to lose speed. Why? In part, obviously, because procedural and semantic become fixed in memory through repetitive encounter. But perhaps also because, in terms of sheer survival, it is not important to remember where you went walking yesterday and whom you met and what you chatted about. What is important to remember is what *walking* means and how to walk.

We no longer *need* full-strength episodic. It would be nice to have, and it drives us crazy when we don't have it, but we no longer need it.

Or take that other mystery, people's names. Why can't we remember them? Well, if you consider it from an evolutionary perspective, why *should* we remember them? Why should we *expect* to remember them? Consider the number of names that come at you in a single day — at home, at work, on the street, on the TV, online, in news-papers, and so on. Each of us probably encounters more people in that one day than a human ever encountered over an entire lifetime, until very, very recently.

In this sense, you might say that evolution hasn't caught up with the realities of modern life. We are a work in progress. Presumably, if we don't blow ourselves up first, we will keep progressing.

Brief detour here for a time line, just to clarify what *very, very recently* means. Planet Earth is said to be about four and a half billion years old, an estimate geologists arrive at by taking rocks apart atom by atom. It is, they say, sort of like estimating a tree's age by counting its rings, though that doesn't sound quite as labor-intensive to me.

Life on Earth, in the form of single-celled microbes, emerged somewhere between two and a half billion and four billion years ago, growing on the sea floor.

Mammals emerged about two hundred million years ago.

Humanoids (as opposed to anthropoids — apes and their kin) emerged between one and two million years ago.

We — Homo sapiens — emerged some-where betwecn forty and a hundred thousand years ago. That is *it*.

So you can see that, in the full mcasure of things, we have not been around for long — let's say, trillionths of a nanosecond (which is a billionth of a second, as I learned about sixty seconds ago) of Earth's existence. But you can also see that, once we started to move, we moved *fast*. And once we began inventing technology, we moved *spectacularly* fast.

For one dizzying example, the futurist Ray Kurzweil tells us in his book *The Age of Spiritual Machines:* "Computers are about one hundred million times more powerful for the same unit cost than they were a half century ago. If the automobile industry had made as much progress in the past fifty years, *a car today would cost a hundredth of a cent and go faster than the speed of light*."

Italics mine. More about the futurists in the next chapter. End of detour.

I told Dr. Jagust that I could understand that, as far as evolution is concerned, all bodily bets are off after childbearing and child-rearing age. I might not like it, but I could understand it — the softening muscles, the shrinking ovaries, the weakening sperm, the works. But why hit us in our memories?

He said, "What we call normal memory loss with aging is really pretty mild. In most cases it doesn't produce serious disabilities."

Then why have it happen at all?

The answer to this one is usually, Because remembering all the unimportant stuff would clutter your mind (the Sherlock Holmes Effect).

But if it would clutter our minds, it would clutter the minds of our children and grandchildren as well. Why pick on *us?* What would be so bad about letting us keep our memories intact?

Considering this question, I could hear the plaintive plea of that lovable little Everyman, Tevye, in the Broadway musical *Fiddler on the Roof.*

He did realize, Tevye told God, that God had made a great many poor people. And he further realized, of course, that it was no big shame to be poor. But it was no big honor, either. Would it have been so bad if God had arranged for him to have a modest fortune?

With apologies to Tevye, one might ask of Mother Nature: I do realize that you made many, many tip-of-the-tonguers. And I realize further that it's no shame, absolutely *not,* to be a tip-of-the-tonguer. But the truth is, it's no great pleasure cither. So: What would be so bad if you had arranged it so that I could remember where the hell I left my glasses?

And the answer came back: It wouldn't be cost-efficient.

Biologically, your body is a morass of cut-throat competitiveness. Zillions of cells are competing to survive. Evolutionary scientists speak of metabolic processes that are "costly" and "expensive" to maintain, of capacities that must "earn their keep" by helping reproduction. If some process becomes so costly that the price of maintaining it outweighs the advantage (an "advantage" being anything that aids reproduction), it gets phased out — in evolutionary jargon, "selected against."

That is natural selection. I think of it as cellular capitalism.

Now, the brain is a supercostly, high-maintenance organ, and its frontal lobes are *especially* high-maintenance. And, as we have seen, they may be essential to episodic memory, but episodic memory is not essential to *us.* So you don't have to be a graduate of the Harvard Business School to grasp the cost-benefit analysis of the thing.

"The frontal lobes are probably the last part of the brain to develop, as well as the first to go," Dr. Jagust said. Last hired, first fired. "Why do they go first? First of all, I don't know." (Question: How often do you hear your medical doctor saying *that?*) "But I think these are reasonable reasons: They get a tremendous amount of input from every other part of the brain. They use a lot of blood flow, a lot of oxygen; they are metabolically expensive to maintain. So it costs all that metabolic energy, and I would say that the amount of benefit the species" (That's us, friends.) "gets from it is not great enough to maintain the fully active function of the system."

Still, I wondered: It may be irrelevant to evolution what happens to *us,* but if the name of the game is to optimize reproductive advantages, wouldn't a child's chance of surviving to reproductive age be greater if she or he had not only Mommy and Daddy's memories to rely on but Grandma and Grandpa's too?

"Oh, yes, that argument has a name," Dr. Jagust said. "It's called the Grandfather Argument."

The Grandfather Argument! Skewered. Here I had assumed that I was doing some nice creative thinking, and instead I had simply lighted, mindless as a bee upon a bush, on a well-known formula called the Grandfather Argument.

"Yes," he said, "that's been one of the arguments raised for healthy aging. But you have to be careful. I don't know what the mean life span was for most of those years that humans like ourselves existed, but my guess is that it was thirty or forty. A grandparent might have been thirty-five years old." In other words, well before the age at which our episodic memory systems start playing peekaboo with us.

There it is, the bottom line: *We were not designed to live so long.*

So how come we do?

The biological anthropologist Terrence Deacon has a nice theory. He does not call it a nice theory. He calls it his wild and crazy hypothesis.

"The classic way to get a mammal to live a long time," he says, "is to cut its diet way back." The diet he is talking about is caloric restriction, which is — well, you must remember caloric restriction. Who could forget caloric restriction? The mouth begins to water at the very thought.

"We do not have that diet. So why do we live so long? At my age," (He is fifty-seven.)

"gorillas and chimpanzees are so senescent that they can't fight off disease, their metabolism has dropped way down, their cognition is probably significantly impaired. Why do we age so much slower and live half again longer than other species that are our size and have other metabolic features like ours? This, I think, is still a mystery. But I do have a hypothesis.

"I think it has to do with our big brains and all that metabolic energy they take. I think that internally our system *thinks,* so to speak, that it is calorie-restricted, because the brain is taking more of its share of energy than it should. I think that our big brains have, in effect, fooled our bodies into aging slowly in order to conserve energy.

"Now, other species with very big brains for their body size have the same feature." As Dr. Deacon speaks, a small dog stirs at his feet. Dr. Jagust had his cat sitting in on the interview, Dr. Deacon has his dog. "I used to have a big black Lab named Max. Max died at a reasonably good age for a big dog, age fifteen. This little Chelsea, here, will probably live to about eighteen or nineteen. Small dogs live longer than big dogs. And the biggest dogs live the shortest lives."

Did you know this? I did not.

"And small dogs have proportionately larger brains?" I asked, being the quick study that I am.

"*Much* larger."

"So a disproportionately large brain, in some sense, mimics caloric restriction."

"That's my wild and crazy hypothesis. I think this aging thing is epiphenomenal." (A phenomenon that occurs alongside, and appears to result from, another phenomenon.) "And it's maintained because our big brains are maintained. This Methuselah consequence, I think, is a free gift of our having this big brain."

A gift. He is not suggesting that evolution endowed us with these big brains *in order for* us to have abnormally long lives — but rather that our abnormally long lives are an accidental by-product of our having these big brains.

What a freebie.

Our brains may be big, but our memories — need I tell you? — are unreliable. Our very *neurons* are unreliable. As Dr. Deacon says, "Hundreds of billions of those little guys in there . . . you know, most of the signals in the brain originate from random metabolic jitter."

There are two schools of thought about

the unreliability of memory.

One is that Mother Nature could have done better. This is the belief of many futurists who hope to improve the design of . . . *us.* They dream — not pie-in-the-sky dreaming but research-in-the-lab dreaming — of building robots that will do what the human memory system does, but better. Much better.

The other is that there is a method in Mother Nature's madness: The imperfections of our memory system are a trade-off for its overall efficiency.

The system has a built-in bias, writes the Tufts University philosopher Daniel C. Dennett, in *Breaking the Spell:* "It has been designed by eons of evolution to remember some sorts of things more readily than others. It does this in part by differential rehearsal, dwelling on what is vital and tending to discard the trivia after a single pass."

Well, this makes perfect sense to me when I can't remember the location of the Sea of Okhotsk, but I have trouble with it when I can't remember the location of my wallet.

The psychologist Daniel L. Schacter takes the trade-off argument a step further, proposing in his book *The Seven Sins of Memory* that the very *failures* of memory may have advantages of their own:

"It is surely infuriating when, operating on automatic pilot, you put down a book or your wallet in an atypical location and later can't remember where you left it. But suppose that when you misplaced the object, you were mentally absorbed in thinking about ways to cut costs in your business, and came up with a great idea that saved you lots of money . . . When we can perform routine tasks by relying on automatic processes, we are free to devote attention to more consequential matters. Because we rely on automatic processes frequently in our daily lives, the occasional absent-minded error seems a relatively small cost for such a large benefit."

I confess that when I read this, the thought did occur to me: Were these really beneficial trade-offs, or was Dr. Schacter looking for the pony in the haystack?

Which was the question I put to him in his office: "Is this really an efficiency of the system, that we forget the kinds of things that we forget?"

He said, "Absolutely. The system is set up so that there is an almost built-in insurance that what is significant and important is what has the best chance of getting stored and getting retrieved. A lot depends on what you think the functions of memory are. *Memory is probably more about the future than it is about the past.*"

This line (again, italics mine) struck me as one that I would *never* forget, and I asked him to elaborate.

"Well," he said, "I don't think that we hold on to our past experiences just to give us a warm and fuzzy feeling about the past. It's to help us anticipate what is going to happen to us next. From that perspective, what is important is to hold on to the *essence* of experience, to extract from it the generalities that occur to you again and again, even if your memory doesn't hold on to all the particulars. Memory, especially episodic memory, helps us plan for, think about, helps us — *simulate* is a word I like to use — helps us *simulate* future possibilities before they actually occur. I think that is one of the key reasons why we have memory at all!"

The crowning achievement of the human species: That is what the philosopher Dennett calls this ability of ours to anticipate what lies ahead. Dennett is talking on a global scale, being able to anticipate the weather, anticipate economic crises, anticipate the state of our oil reserves decades in advance — all huge, urgent prognostications.

But the same is true of our *individual* ability to anticipate — it is a crowning achievement. And it rests, of course, upon memory. We are able to plan for the future because we are able to remember the past.

Dr. Schacter gave me a dramatic example of the link between past and future. He and the renowned Canadian psychologist, Endel Tulving, once were interviewing a severely amnesiac patient, a man who could remember nothing of his past. Schacter asked him what he was planning to do the following day, "and he just drew a complete and utter blank. He could not come up with anything. Absolutely unable to provide any information at all.

"You know, we might think, Yeah, sure, amnesiac patients, they can't remember the past but they can think about the future, right? But what does it mean to think about what you're going to do tomorrow? Partly, you've got to draw on your memory of recent experiences — what you've been doing, what kind of thing you are likely to do. You have to be able to pull out the kind of information from your recent past that allows you to think about tomorrow and next week and next year."

So we are back to the same central question: If it is especially episodic memory that helps us do this extraordinary thing, why mess with our episodic memory?

And to the same central answer: "Things that happen later in life tend to be affected less by evolutionary pressures than things that happen earlier, before childbearing age."

And thus, again, to that same old bottom line: We were not designed to live so long.

But take note: The center holds. The system works. Irritating as normal memory loss may be, the system's tilt toward what is vital, a bias built into us over eons of evolution, stays intact.

Which is to say, you may forget *yet again* where you put your reading glasses, or the keys to your car, or your wallet, but you remember full well how to read and how to drive and how to spend or save or count or worry about whatever is or is not in that wallet that you cannot find.

Accidents happen. We are perambulations of accident. We evolve by chance, in a process that is not unlike Dr. Deacon's palimpsest model of memory, each version of ourselves layered upon the prior version. It is a process of *evolving* toward greater efficiency — efficiency meaning the ability to reproduce and to care for offspring until they themselves can reproduce — and in the course of this process there are bum moves, bad directions, fluky fits and starts, all blind, all pure chance. Biological mutations pop up for no apparent reasons, memories make — as we know so well — stupid mistakes (intelligent mistakes, some cognitive scientists call them, which is a cheering thought), genes go off on random walks.

That phrase, *random walks:* It has a casual stroll-around-the-block kind of sound, but in fact it is a term scientists use. If there is no selective advantage for something, the genes simply begin to take a random walk.

I first heard the term from Berkeley's Dr. Deacon. "Let me give you an example," he said. "You and I need vitamin C. We get it from fruit. That's because we're primates. Most other mammals make their own vitamin C. And they do so because it's a critical molecule to protect against oxidative damage.

"A group of Japanese researchers published a paper in 1994 that identified the gene that enables rats to produce their own vitamin C. Then they used this gene as a probe to look for its homologue — its evolutionary cousin — in other species. Surprisingly, though we can't produce our own vitamin C, they discovered that *we* have a *pseudo*-vitamin-C-producing gene that has been shut off.

"Well, it was almost certainly shut off because, about thirty-five million years ago, our ancestors, the monkeys and apes, began to eat fruit. So then, because vitamin C was constantly available, the gene producing it didn't matter. So defects began to accumulate in the lineage. And when a gene has been randomly damaged enough, you can't repair it, because it would have to be repaired randomly, too.

"So what the random walk means is, you start from a specific place — in this case, a specific sequence in the DNA — and you just sort of slowly wander away from that point. Initially, there may not have been significant disadvantage. A few mutations took place in that gene that still didn't destroy its function. But over time, you (the gene) walked further and further away. It's sometimes called a drunkard's walk: It starts in one place, and it just randomly wanders around, and gets progressively further and further from that starting point.

"That notion of random walk is characteristic of what we see when natural selection stops, which it did in this case because we were getting vitamin C *from the outside.* Then the genes begin to accumulate mutations at random, eventually stop working, and you end up with a pseudo gene."

From the outside! I think this raises an unsettling question. Not that it's keeping me up nights, but it is unsettling.

When I'm stuck in the middle of a crossword puzzle because I can't remember — if, indeed, I ever knew — the Latin word for *elbow* or what Theodore Roosevelt's wife's name was, I go to Google. Meaning that I get the answer *from the outside.* (In a word, I cheat.)

So my question is: Is it possible that far, far down the line, brain cells will start wandering off, taking a random walk, getting lost, going to hell, becoming *pseudo* cells, because our descendants are getting their memory *from the outside?*

The futurists are working on it. As we will now see.

CHAPTER SEVENTEEN:
BEYOND THE BOTOX
GENERATION

MEMORY AND TOMORROW

The most curious part of the thing was, that the trees and the other things round them never changed their places at all: however fast they went, they never seemed to pass anything . . .

"Are we nearly there?" Alice managed to pant out at last.

"Nearly there!" the Queen repeated. "Why, we passed it ten minutes ago! Faster!"

— Lewis Carroll, *Through the Looking-Glass*

It didn't turn out the way it was supposed to, folks.

Back in the Stone Age of technology, in 1970, the futurist writer Alvin Toffler predicted that by the year 2000 we would all be working less, relaxing more, lolling in hammocks and trying to figure out what to do with all that free time.

Didn't quite happen. What happened

instead was economic globalization. The competitive pace quickened to a gallop. People found themselves working more, relaxing less, complaining endlessly about not getting enough sleep — the endemic American complaint — and finding that they must move faster just to keep up.

It's what evolutionary biologists, when they describe the pressure on competing species to survive, call the Red Queen principle: in *Through the Looking-Glass,* Alice and the Red Queen keep running hard but getting nowhere. Alice is befuddled, and the Queen explains: "It takes all the running *you* can do, to keep in the same place. If you want to get somewhere else, you must run at least twice as fast as that!"

And where will it go from here? Will the rat race ease off or become even faster? Here is a big, big clue: In that same year of 1970, according to the Census Bureau, most college freshmen said that their primary personal goal was "to develop a meaningful philosophy of life."

In 2005, according to the Bureau's 2007 Statistical Abstract, most college freshmen said that their primary personal goal was "to be financially very well off."

We've come a long way, baby.

"I talk to a lot of boomers," the neurologist Adam Gazzaley tells me in his office at the University of California, San Francisco, where he is the director of the neuroscience imaging laboratory. "Keeping sharper longer — we know how much that means to boomers. Some of them just turned sixty, and they want to continue working. They want to compete. They are trying to compete with thirty-year-olds, and keeping their brains healthy so they can perform on a cognitive level that lets them stay competitive — that is really important to them."

It is not so easy to compete with the thirty-year-olds when you have trouble doing several tasks at once and you can't always remember the names that go with those new (baby) faces in the office and you can't find your notes from yesterday's meeting, which would not do you much good even if you could find them, because you can't find your glasses, either.

A dilemma. What is to be done?

"It might come down to some kinds of interventions," Dr. Gazzaley says, "some potential ways that we may be able to improve those abilities that we know are changing as people's brains change with aging."

Interventions. Meaning tools, external to ourselves, for improving upon our mortally imperfect design.

Meaning that what Mother Nature has not done for memory, technology may yet do instead.

Of course, interventions already abound. We have rehabilitative interventions for most every part of the human body. There is Botox for the wrinkled forehead. There is Rogaine for the balding scalp. There is Viagra for the recalcitrant penis. There is what is odiously called *pink* Viagra, to do for women's sex drive what Viagra does for men's. (Although as of this writing it is not on the market because it does not work, and it does not work because women's sexual arousal works differently from men's, a fact that the drug makers spent years and God knows how many research dollars discovering. A pity. Any woman could have told them.)

We have surgical cosmetic interventions for the face, the neck, the ears, the arms, the legs, the breasts, the belly, the buttocks, the genitals (don't ask), the works. High time, then, for the brain.

I live near Manhattan's Central Park, can see it from my windows, can see the joggers incessantly circling the reservoir in downpours, in heat waves, weather be damned.

On nearby city blocks, I pass workout centers. I peer through windows, see the rows of red-faced exercisers upon their stationary bikes and elliptical trainers, all occupied, all hours of day and night. Many if not most of them look to be in their early boomer years. Sometimes I wonder, Who are those people? Don't they work?

Probably. But you can always make time for what you really, *really* want to do.

We have been, for three decades and more, a physical-exercise-crazed culture. Now we seem to be on the cusp of a cultural sea change. Not that the physical-fitness mania is dropping off but that a mental-fitness mania is overtaking it. Fads come and go in the field of health as in every other, in one era and out the next, like skirt lengths. We are entering — already have entered, though what we have today is probably a bag of stale peanuts compared to what we will have tomorrow — a mental-exercise-crazed era.

I see four big reasons for it. There must be others, but these are the four that seem most persuasive to me:

1. The great revolution caused by brain-scan technology that makes it possible for neuroscientists to see

how our brains work and explore ways to make them work better.

2. The baby boomers' fear of dementia and fixation on staying mentally sharp.

3. Disposable income: Boomers have it and spend it, controlling seventy percent of the nation's wealth and spending more than any generation in our history.

4. Profit: The pure genius of our health-industrial complex for turning, wherever and however possible, a dollar.

Put all these together, and they do not spell Mother. They spell Anti-Aging Industry.

Where neuroscience leads, commerce will follow. So, keeping in mind the perils of prediction, let us see where neuroscience *appears* to be leading.

Here are the interventions of tomorrow:

Brain exercise: interactive computer programs tailored to individual needs. Old-style strategies taught you how to *compensate* for the memory losses that come with age-related brain changes. These new ones aim to *rehabilitate* your brain.

You can start each day with a brisk brain workout at your computer before heading for the office.

"Smart pills": drugs to improve your memory and general cognition by chemically boosting the neurotransmission systems of your brain.

Invasive procedures: various electrical and chemical manipulations to sharpen your good memories, blunt the bad ones, and even — are you ready? — leave you with glorious memories of experiences that you never actually had.

Genetic interventions: manipulation of genes that are linked to memory. Still on the drawing board, though they have been doing, successfully, plenty of genetic fooling around with laboratory mice.

Brain implants: a computer chip implanted into the head, onto which you can download . . . whatever.

Which means, in effect and in reality, that you now have a memory backup system.
Cool.

First, brain exercise — also called brain training, brain calisthenics, brain fitness, cognitive training, cognitive rehabilitation, and such and so. No need to wait for tomorrow. A relatively crude forerunner is already, inescapably, here.

Mind-challenging video and computer games have been around for ages, but they hadn't been marketed as *therapeutic,* and they certainly hadn't been marketed to our demographic. Then, several years back, came a couple of widely publicized studies which indicated that training exercises actually can improve the memory of people who have normal, age-related memory loss.

Add to this a statistic that some anonymous number cruncher came up with: *Every eight seconds, another baby boomer turns fifty.* Another tip-of-the-tonguer joins the club!

Well, you can imagine. Combine those studies and that statistic, and they created a climate of opportunity that no sane toy and/or game manufacturer could reasonably be expected to ignore. Suddenly they had a huge new market — *us!* — and what started as a trend quickly became a rage.

Time magazine, in a January 2007 report headlined "A Nintendo for Grandma," noted, "The over-50 set is a largely untapped and potentially lucrative market, and toy and gaming companies are starting to court the boomer generation with products claiming to help sharpen memory and cognitive ability."

A front-page *New York Times* story in December 2006, waxed cautiously hyperbolic: "Science is not sure yet, but across the country, brain health programs are springing up, offering the possibility of a cognitive fountain of youth."

Brain Age, Brain Boost, Train Your Brain, Love Your Brain, Brain Fitness, MindFit, Happy Neuron, Ultimate Brain Games, Big Brain Academy . . . the Internet was swiftly overrun with video games and Web site programs. "Brain fitness centers" and "brain gyms" and "brain workshops" were installed in community facilities, hospital clinics, senior citizens' centers, retirement communities, assisted-living complexes, nursing homes, and in halls of commerce where corporations inaugurated brain-exercise programs for their employees (voluntary, at least for now; tomorrow, who knows?).

From Nintendo, maker of Pokémon, now came Brain Age: Train Your Brain in Minutes a Day! (600,000 units sold in the first eight months), based, we were told, on the research of a Japanese neuroscientist. From Mattel, maker of Barbie dolls, came Brain Games, based, we were told, on the research of a University of California psychiatrist (who touts his own "pioneering strategies" to improve memory, though basically those pioneering strategies seem to be at least two thousand years old).

Everything, we were told, was based on some scientist's research. The problem was neatly posed by an officer of the American Society on Aging: "The challenge we have is, it's going to be a lot like the anti-aging industry: How much science is there behind this?"

Good question.

The largest national study of brain exercise, reported in the *Journal of the American Medical Association,* had shown that memory training in such tasks as recalling lists of words and details of stories, did, indeed, make a difference. By doing memory exercises, the trainees became more skilled in *doing memory exercises.* But there was little evidence that those skills translated into generally better memory in everyday living. And none that such training can help prevent dementia.

"Can you improve memory with training? Resoundingly, *yes,*" Johns Hopkins's Dr. Barry Gordon tells me. "We know that. What is totally unknown is how far training one mental function in a computer game will take you in the game of life. Probably the kind of mental exercise you would have to do to really improve brain function would be so exhausting and pervasive that people won't think of it as exercise. They'll think of it as living."

Dr. Elizabeth Edgerly, a clinical psychologist with the Alzheimer's Association, told *The New York Times:* "All of the things are good for you to do in general. Do I have concerns? Yes. We're very cautious. Is it going to mean you can remember where you left your car keys? We can't say that."

In other words, Yes, of course, absolutely do the brain-training exercises if you want. (Or design your own. Some game manufacturers stress the fact that their products "exercise different brain functions." So does reading a good book.) Do them because you enjoy them. Do them because they make you feel sharper. Do them because they make you feel virtuous. Do them because they *may* really help — as with dietary supplements, the jury is still out — and they certainly can't hurt. Just don't do them expecting to remember where you left your car keys or glasses, and you won't be disappointed.

Much that is sold now is Mickey Mouse stuff, video games jazzed up and largely untested by scientific standards. But some computer-software companies have been working with labs such as Dr. Gazzaley's, developing exercise programs with increasingly sophisticated interactions between brains and computers, and there are promising early results. He explains how the interaction works:

"The brain is hooked up to our recording information so we are able to see from second to second what is occurring inside the brain while the person interacts with the visual world. If the visual world is a cognitive-training exercise, we can see how the brain is affected by this interaction — how the brain's normal way of working is changed by the training exercise. We feed that information right into the software. So the computer is learning directly about how your brain is acting, and automatically adjusts itself to fine-tuning that brain process."

The researchers are fine-tuning, too. They don't really understand yet precisely how these brain-computer interactions may work, because they don't understand precisely how memory works. But the many I have interviewed are certain that this is where the future of memory rehabilitation lies: in computer training programs — and in what is delicately called pharmacological intervention.

What are "smart pills," exactly?

It turns out that the *exactly* is trickier than we might think. Porous borders. As Dr. Gazzaley draws them:

"A drug that keeps you awake and alert, or a drug that makes you sleep if you have trouble sleeping, so you can perform better the next day — is that a 'smart drug'? If you have depression and you are treated so that you are not depressed anymore, and can focus better, you're going to be 'smarter.' Does that make an antidepressant a 'smart drug'? In a way, it does. So I think that anything that improves well-being in some way could be considered a 'smart drug.' "

By that definition, of course, we are already up to our ears in smart drugs. Check any college campus. But if they make you "smarter," they do so incidentally. These new pills, which may be as common as aspirin by 2018, if not long before, are a whole other story. They will be aimed specifically at making you smarter by improving your memory and general cognition, which they will probably do by chemically boosting — recharging, you might call it — those trillions of connections amid the billions of neural networks that weaken in the normal course of aging.

On paper, such pills will be strictly for therapeutic use. Pharmaceutical houses don't like to talk about the prospect of cosmetic use, which often is called cosmetic neurology. The reason they don't like to talk about it is that the Food and Drug Administration only approves drugs to treat sickness, not to ice the cake for healthy people.

And so you get a kind of peekaboo effect, as in the conspicuous case of Viagra. As *The New York Times* has noted: "Pfizer has always straddled a line marketing Viagra, insisting that the drug treats a serious medical condition, impotence, and deserves insurance coverage, while promoting the drug with wink-and-a-nod ads that have irritated regulators."

So what the drug houses will be stressing with smart drugs will be help for people with significant cognitive damage. But it is the slipperiest slope this side of an Alpine ski run, and everybody knows that when these pills become available, if they can make people who have razor-sharp minds just a little quicker on the uptake, people with razor-sharp minds will want them. Avidly.

No one (well, hardly anyone) quarrels

with using demonstrably safe drugs to help people who need help, and the primary hope, of course, is for a drug to cure or treat Alzheimer's. But this issue of *cosmetic* use raises questions that have caused a firestorm of debate in professional circles: Is it ethical? "Do you take people who are functioning at a perfectly good level and make them 'smarter'? That's what's not clear," Dr. Gazzaley says.

And, further, will what constitutes "a perfectly good level" today still cut the mustard tomorrow? I hear the echo of that comment from Dr. Norman Relkin, head of the Memory Disorders Program at Cornell University: "It is said that what's normal in one generation becomes pathology and disease in the next. This thing that we're calling normal forgetfulness will probably not be acceptable in another generation or two."

And what about people who just don't want to mess around with chemicals, not for themselves and not for their children — will they be disadvantaged? *Pop a pill, get a promotion, ace an exam. Don't pop, get left behind.*

And what about "forgetfulness pills" for painful emotional memories? It would be nice to rid ourselves of them, but at what cost? Our memories, after all, do make us who we are. Imagine the slippery slope on *that* one: Feeling a pinch of embarrassment, a dash of regret, a wisp of envy or sadness or rue? *No problem,* chum. Pop a pill.

"Sometimes I wish I had one of those pills," the neurologist Judy Illes says. A professor at the University of British Columbia, she previously headed the neuroethics program at Stanford University and is prominent in the ethics debate. "The temptation to speed up on my efficiency to get it all done is huge. But then I think: 'If I do that, when am I *me?*'

"The challenges begin with questions about identity. But safety, fair access to resources for people of all walks of life, and the intangible but inescapable question of the value of hard work and authenticity — they all factor in to make enhancement a challenging arena for debate."

And as to safety, what if it turned out to be not simply *not nice,* but disastrous, to fool Mother Nature? Might drugs improve one vital memory function at the expense of another, or cram our brains with the very sorts of trivia that we have been programmed to ignore?

I e-mailed these questions to Terrence Deacon soon after interviewing him at the

University of California, Berkeley, and he answered: "There are always trade-offs, and the power of natural selection is that it takes all integrated functioning into account, not just one function, in evolving an organism. We fiddle with the balance at some peril unless we understand how the whole system works."

But none of the questions kicks up more ethical dust than this: In a society where the gap between haves and have-nots keeps widening, would the new generation of smart pills simply widen it further?

When those drugs come to market, you may be sure that they will be, at least in the beginning, very expensive. And you may also be sure that solvent boomers with normal memory loss will be lined up to buy them, and so will their children, just to get that extra edge, and so will hordes of young parents who will want their toddlers primed to compete for places in the right nursery school, which leads to the right private middle school, which leads to the right Ivy League college, which leads . . .

But you know where it leads. It's always the same old deal. The Red Queen principle, in spades.

Many scientists take a purely pragmatic position: Their research may produce a product that brings help to people who desperately need help. And if it also gets used cosmetically — well, that's the reality throughout society, anyway: People with money have an advantage, and what else is new? We don't prohibit cosmetic work on their bodies, how can we discriminate against their brains?

Difficult, difficult questions. But will any of them stall the forward march of cosmetic neurology?

You must be kidding.

People who would reach eagerly for the smart pills might be far less eager to try the invasive procedures. Such as:

Electrical energizers inserted under the scalp to provide continuous stimulation and thus, theoretically, aid memory. This procedure is already in use to treat depression, and I have heard it rumored that somewhere in the tangled heart of Manhattan is a surgeon who uses it for memory, and also gives massages and pedicures on the side. I didn't check it out. I couldn't bear to know.

Surgical manipulations to boost aging brains (brain lifts, one surgeon jauntily calls them).

And the beckoning possibility of one day being able to implant into the brain, by direct chemical injection, a totally artificial memory.

What kind of memory? Why, any kind you like. Choose from the menu: romance, drama, action, mystery, comedy . . .

It sounds pure sci-fi, but not much sci is pure fi anymore. Researchers at the Massachusetts Institute of Technology, who are working on the manipulation of memory in rats, speculate that one day, a man may be able to order up a memory of having spent a divine night with Marilyn Monroe. They call it the Marilyn Monroe experiment. They can call it whatever they like, but I see no reason to be bound by the limits of their thinking. I'll call it the George Clooney experiment. Now, *that's* what I call an intervention.

> More and more, memory is becoming external. Most boomers will end up part human and part machine.
> — Rodney Brooks, Panasonic Professor of Robotics, Massachusetts Institute of Technology

I nearly fell out of my seat when he said that. But then, tomorrow is today at MIT.

When we met, Rodney Brooks was the director of MIT's Computer Science and

Artificial Intelligence Laboratory. Soon after, he resigned from the directorship to devote himself full-time to robotics research. Brooks works out of a suitably spectacular building designed by the California architect Frank Gehry, who put a chimney flue through the vaulted roof of the laboratory and told him, "When you get a great idea, send up a wisp of white smoke."

As distinguished as anyone alive in the field of artificial intelligence — AI, as we aficionados say — Brooks could probably send up a smoke signal a day. Here is this affable, laidback, transplanted Aussie who seems as down-to-earth as you can imagine, and then he gets going, begins to describe what they do under this roof, and what they want to do, and it is totally off the planet. Or so it sounds to an earthling like me.

A big part of what they do here is face the music, demographically speaking: the reality that more and more of us will be living longer and longer, while technology keeps giving us more and more to remember (think of access codes and passwords *alone*), and thus more and more to forget.

Brooks and his team are seeking ways to help us cope with an incomprehensible volume of information. "How you make sense of it. How you search for stuff, how

you find stuff, how you remember stuff —
how you live in a world with all this information that is not confusing and is coherent
and makes life better."

And how do we do that? What does it
mean to say that, more and more, memory
is becoming external?

"In the old days," he says, "you had to
keep everything in your head. All history
was oral. Then came books, and people
didn't have to remember everything. Then,
in the twentieth century, with the rise of
newspapers, and books becoming cheap, it
completely changed the expectation of how
much you needed to store in your head. You
had it in your home. And now there is so
much stuff, so instantly available on the
Web, that we no longer feel a need to have
it in our homes. Once we might have gone
to the encyclopedia." (As we still do in my
home. There they sit, all twenty-three
volumes, a noble, antediluvian lineup on a
den shelf. We do our googling and marvel at
its wonders, but how dandy it is to take
down one of those volumes, feel its heft,
thumb its pages, stroke its fine yellowing
paper. How much tactile pleasure is there
in a computer screen?) "Now we're all
googling stuff all the time. And so, what
used to have to fit in my brain simply got

too big. So I get it out of the Web. And the tools we have to do that are fairly primitive, I think, compared to where they might go in future — to where I *hope* they will go."

Brooks tells me of a colleague, the purest of pure of the futurists, who believes that in twenty years he will be able to download his own consciousness — meaning every last trace of memory buried within him — onto a machine.

"I think he goes too far," Brooks says fondly, "but he believes it. So he has to eat healthy, live healthy, live long enough to get his eternal salvation downloaded. It's eternal life for atheists!"

His own vision of tomorrow follows two main avenues of research: computer science (meaning, essentially, brain implants) and AI (meaning, essentially, robots).

As to robots, he passionately holds a view widely held among futurists. You may call it thrilling, you may call it terrifying, but nobody can call it boring. In essence: Human beings are machines made out of molecules, and thus it should be possible — *in principle,* which is a phrase he keeps stressing — to make robots out of synthesized molecules. Robots with intelligence and emotion. Robots with a human memory system (but improved) built into them. The ultimate memory backup system.

"Can you synthesize all the molecules that make us up?" I asked.

"I think it's fairly likely that we will be able to. But whether we could put them together in the right form, whether we are smart enough to do that, is the question."

"And if you could, emotional intelligence would be built into this machine?"

"Certainly. In principle."

"You believe it could feel the enjoyment that I feel now, listening to you?"

"I would hope so. We have been getting beaten up by science for the last thousand years. Science keeps eating away at our specialness. What was the Galileo debate about? Well, in part, about the idea that God made the world for *us*. Earth was the center of the universe. Galileo said, 'No, no, we go around the sun!' People said, 'We go around the sun? That can't be right! That is terrible!' Now we say, 'We're part of the animal kingdom? That can't be right! We're special!'

"When Garry Kasparov, the chess champion, was beaten by Deep Blue, the IBM machine, do you remember what he said? He said, 'Well, at least it didn't *enjoy* beating me.' That cold, calculating machine — it couldn't enjoy like *he* could. And so you say, 'Do you think a robot could enjoy listening like *I* can?' You know, we want to be special."

At which point, I took a flier: "Forgive me an impertinence?"

"Absolutely."

"You're in bed with your wife."

"Yes."

"You're making love."

"Yes."

"You reach a climax."

"Yes."

"Do you think — *in principle* — a computer would be able to replicate that experience?"

"In principle? Yes! My wife might not want it in bed with her, but . . . yes!"

What greets the visitor now in the Humanoid Robotics Laboratory is a company of robots that look neither humanoid nor robotic but more like a Rube Goldberg contraption. My previous images of robots having come exclusively from Hollywood, these are a big surprise.

They are maybe two feet in height, with extensions that are loosely — very loosely — equivalent to a head and torso and limbs, and their zillions of parts are fully exposed: gears, cables, springs, motors, circuit boards, wires, mechanical and electrical whatnots, assemblages put together out of some hardware store on the Moon. And there has been no effort to make them in any way humanoid-looking — except for one, which has a cartoon kind of smiley-baby face and a sign beneath it that reads: "Hello, my name is Mertz. Please interact with me. I am trying to learn to recognize different people."

Brooks has a wish list for his robots:

"The first thing I want is the object-recognition capabilities of a two-year-old child. Because a two-year-old can come into a place they've never been before, look at objects they've never seen before, and name them.

"Next, the language capabilities of a four-year-old.

"Next, the manual dexterity of a six-year-old. A six-year-old can tie shoelaces and do everything that a factory worker has the manual dexterity to do.

"And then, the social understanding of an eight-year-old. An eight-year-old can distinguish between what a person says and what that person believes."

"What about a capacity for memory, being able to retain and retrieve?" I ask, and it is clear from his expression that I have missed the boat.

"Well, you need *all* of that for the two-year-old," he says.

"So the whole wish list presupposes memory?"

"Absolutely!"

Mertz keeps smiling.

Whether a robot with a human memory system ever comes to pass, it certainly will not come to pass for *us.* But brain implants? Those are in the foreseeable future.

Brooks starts out slow: "I use an iPod as a memory device. A four-hundred-dollar iPod. In 2003, for that four hundred dollars, you got a ten gigabyte iPod. In 2004 you got a twenty gig, in 2005 a forty gig, in 2006 an eighty gig. It doubles every year. By 2013, the whole Library of Congress will fit on an iPod. By 2020, every movie ever made, every TV show, will fit on an iPod. We will be able to carry our entire memory of past entertainment in our pockets. People my age" (He is fifty-three.) "will be reminiscing, 'What about that time Lucy said to Ricky . . . ,' and we'll find that particular episode on our iPods."

That is pretty impressive external memory. But what does it do for our overworked *internal* memories, besides lighten the load?

"Okay, now let's get a little weird," he

says. "There are a hundred thousand people in the world today who have chips in their heads because they went deaf and got cochlear implants. A computer in the head connects to the nerves in the ear, and now they can hear again. There is research in macular degeneration, and a few people now have chips implanted in their retinas, and others have external cameras connected to chips implanted in the visual cortex.

"I can see, within the next twenty years, more of that technology giving us access to memory. Now we go to the computer and google for the information we want. But let's imagine that we may just *think* it in the future. Let's imagine that by having connections in our language centers and a virtual Web browser in our visual cortex, we may just *think* what we want to search and have the results appear in our minds — in the same way people just *hear* stuff because of a computer connected to a microphone implanted in the brain.

"Now, when I talk about this, people say, 'Oh, no, it's only a deaf person who would do this because they want to hear again. People wouldn't just put a chip in their brain if they didn't *have* to.' And you know what I say? I say: Botox! You know — people will do *anything.*"

I have a relative, himself a computer scientist, who used to be a walking international movie database. Recently, he said to me, "I always had this extraordinary memory for trivia. I would remember who was the third director on *Gone with the Wind*. Now I just look it up. At work, nobody takes notes on scientific papers anymore. We just google and find what we need. Which is great, but the downside is what's happened to my memory. It just isn't as good anymore."

Well, I love to google. It enchants me. It boggles my old-fashioned mind how all that stuff got *in* there. But there is a question that nags at me, and I have been so preoccupied for so long with this memory business that I can't get it out of my thoughts.

Question: As the technological pace quickens, isn't it written in the stars that our children (probably) and grandchildren (certainly) will know more but remember less than we ever did? Perhaps, ultimately, they won't have to remember a damned thing.

Which is okay, I suppose, if they can go to that virtual Web browser in their brains to find out whatever they need. As in: *That woman coming toward me, what's her name? Okay, now, downloading, downloading . . .*

Aha! SUSIE!

The prospect has its charms. But it does nag at me.

Rodney Brooks has a good answer. People always worry about progress, he says. It's how we are. "We've been changing in our technology for thousands of years, and there has always been this fear that somehow it's going to make things worse — and in some way, it does. You and I would be hard put if we were left in a cave somewhere and had to make our own fire."

Translation: So, would you rather be back in the cave?

A rhetorical question.

But hold on. This chip that would be imbedded in my skull, doing all my remembering for me — can it feel? Can it call up the joy associated with this particular memory in my (natural) head, and the sadness associated with that one? Can it remember the sensation of pleasure, or hilarity, or curiosity?

Can it remember love?

If so, I would consider it.

Not that I am ungrateful for the memory that Mother Nature and several million years of evolution have bestowed upon me, warts and all. Listen, I am devoutly grateful.

Here's to Mother Nature.

Here's to evolution.

Here's to memory — to yours and to mine, and to Whatsisname's too.

But oh, how sweet it would be never again to have to say, *"Where did I leave my glasses?"*

ABOUT THE AUTHOR

Martha Weinman Lear has written two books, *Heartsounds* and *The Child Worshipers,* and scores of articles for national magazines.

Her memoir, *Heartsounds,* the story of her late husband, the surgeon Harold Lear, his odyssey as a doctor-turned-patient, and the effect of that odyssey upon their marriage, was a *New York Times* bestseller and became required reading in many medical schools across the country.

Ms. Lear is a former articles editor and staff writer with *The New York Times Magazine.* She has written extensively on social and medicine-related topics.

She lives in New York with her husband, the screenwriter Albert Ruben, and says that, as best she can recall, they have no pets.

The employees of Thorndike Press hope you have enjoyed this Large Print book. All our Thorndike and Wheeler Large Print titles are designed for easy reading, and all our books are made to last. Other Thorndike Press Large Print books are available at your library, through selected bookstores, or directly from us.

For information about titles, please call:
    (800) 223-1244

or visit our Web site at:
    http://gale.cengage.com/thorndike

To share your comments, please write:
    Publisher
    Thorndike Press
    295 Kennedy Memorial Drive
    Waterville, ME 04901